BOUNCE ***FORWARD***

21 TOOLS TO LIVE A LIFE ***BEYOND LIMITS***

AMY PURDY

www.amplifypublishinggroup.com

Bounce Forward: 21 Tools to Live a Life Beyond Limits

For more information, please contact:
Amplify Publishing, an imprint of Amplify Publishing Group
620 Herndon Parkway, Suite 220
Herndon, VA 20170
info@amplifypublishing.com

Library of Congress Control Number: 2025926077

CPSIA Code: PRFRE0126A

ISBN-13: 979-8-89138-636-5

Printed in Canada

To the person facing a challenge—
whether it's a challenge you chose
or a challenge that chose you.
May these pages be a compass through the unknown,
not guiding you back to who you once were
but forward into who you are becoming.

Contents

Part Two: FORWARD

INTRODUCTION

If you want to hear God laugh, tell him your plans.
—Proverb

AT THE AGE OF NINETEEN, I was working my dream job as a massage therapist at the world-class Canyon Ranch Spa in Las Vegas. I had big plans—but on July 15, 1999, everything changed.

A few hours after arriving at work, I was hit with a wave of fatigue. As the day wore on, I felt like I was coming down with the flu. By the next morning, I was so sick and weak that I could hardly sit up. When I finally managed to stand, I realized that I couldn't feel my feet. I looked down and saw that my feet and lower legs were purple—and when I glanced in the mirror, I realized that my nose, chin, cheeks, and hands were purple too. My heart pounded in my ears, my vision tunneled, and my body began to shake. I was dying, and I knew it.

Luckily, my cousin stopped by to check on me. Thank God she did. She rushed me to the hospital while I fought to stay awake in the passenger seat. Although I didn't know it at the time, I was in a state of septic shock. Soon after I arrived at the hospital, doctors gave me a less than 2 percent chance of survival. Five days later, they confirmed that I had contracted meningococcal (bacterial) meningitis, one of the deadliest blood infections in the world.

With my family by my side, doctors induced a coma and hooked me up to life support. My kidneys had shut down completely, and I was placed on round-the-clock dialysis to filter toxins from my blood. But that was only the start. While I was in the coma, my organs started failing. I developed a condition known as disseminated intravascular coagulation, or DIC, which thins the blood to the point that even a needle prick can cause hemorrhage. Lying on the operating table, I had a near-death experience in which my heart raced up to 266 beats per minute and I flatlined on the operating table.

For the next two and a half months, I fought for my life. During that fight I ended up losing both of my legs below the knees, my hearing in my left ear, my spleen, my kidney function, and the life I once knew.

But I kept on going. In fact, over the next twenty years, I did more than just bounce back—I bounced forward into a life more beautiful and meaningful than I ever could have imagined.

I learned to walk with two prosthetic legs and run on running blades. I became a professional snowboarder, a three-time Paralympic medalist, the founder of an incredible organization called Adaptive Action Sports, one of the most globally in-demand motivational speakers, a *New York Times* bestselling author of *On My Own Two Feet*, a runner-up on the hit ABC TV show *Dancing with the Stars*, the cofounder of a nonprofit organization dedicated to helping people with disabilities get involved in action sports, the CEO of a seven-figure business, and a wife to an amazingly loving and supportive man. Ironically, it took losing my legs to get there!

If I had merely tried to resume the life I'd been living before getting sick, I might have gone on to be a happy and successful massage therapist. But had I never gone through what I did, I never would have lived the life I have now.

I bounced forward by rebuilding my life piece by piece—my body, my confidence, and everything else. And I found a way to become an even better version of myself than I'd previously believed I could be.

Early on in my recovery, when I was still in my twenties, I would get invited to speak at schools. The organizers would always say, "Just share your story and tell the students how you got through your challenges." Although these words were meant to reassure me and make it sound easy, a knot would form in my throat, and I'd begin to panic. I'd think, *I don't know how I got through my challenges. I just did.* How could I teach people how to do a thing that had just sort of . . . happened?

As I became more well known, the same questions kept popping up. Almost every day someone would ask me, "Amy, how did you make it through your darkest days?" or "How did you go on to thrive even though you were dealing with such hardships?"

For a long time, I didn't really know how to answer these questions. Sometimes, when you're too close to an experience, it's hard to analyze it for the actionable takeaways other people can reproduce for themselves. (And sometimes, when you're too far removed from an experience, you're too disconnected from the hardship to remember how you got through it.)

However, after a few years of reflecting, writing, and learning to share my story in public, I eventually began to understand that we don't just overcome adversity by staying positive and keeping our chin up (though that helps). There are techniques. Practices. Tools. If I truly wanted to help others, I needed to take a closer look at the challenges I faced and document the practices that helped me through them. I started identifying the specific techniques that had helped me bounce forward and sharing them with my audiences.

As the years went on, however, I began to feel more and more distant from the struggle. I'd done such a good job of bouncing forward that I could scarcely remember the depths of despair I'd once faced. I'd crafted a wonderful life—so wonderful that it took a real effort to summon memories of what it felt like to suffer and feel afraid.

What I didn't know was that life was about to gut-punch me with a reminder.

—

In January 2019, I was traveling the world, giving talks and snowboarding. My fortieth birthday was coming up, and I was in the best shape of my life.

The spring before, I'd won my second and third Paralympic medals in snowboarding in PyeongChang, South Korea. At the time, these victories made me the most-medaled Paralympic snowboarder in the history of Team USA.

After years of training at an elite level and fine-tuning my prosthetic legs and equipment, I was snowboarding at my absolute best. For the first time in my entire adult life, my prosthetic legs felt like second nature to me. Most days, I forgot I was even wearing them. I did have some limitations, but I'd adapted to them so well that walking and snowboarding felt as natural as breathing.

It had taken twenty years of constant commitment, practice, and tinkering with equipment and physics to get here—and I'd made it. Between my athletic victories and my jet-setting life giving keynote speeches to as many as thirty thousand people at a time, I felt like I was on top of the world.

Then came the gut punch.

In February 2019, I suffered a life-altering injury to my left leg, and the surgeons told me I'd be lucky to walk to my mailbox again.

If you had asked me what my biggest nightmare was, this would have been it. Losing everything I'd fought for. Being thrown into a sea of uncertainty again. Fighting for my ability to walk—again. Having to rebuild myself—*again.*

And yet here I was.

Ever since I'd survived meningitis, I'd been sure my purpose in life was to push physical limits. Now I was back to asking, *Who am I?* and *What is my purpose now?*

Twenty years ago, when I'd lost my legs, I'd never asked, *Why me?* But faced with this new injury, the question consumed me. *Why me? Why again? Why do I have to endure yet another terrifying and life-altering experience?*

Then, one day in 2024, a stranger told me a story that changed everything.

I was in San Diego delivering a keynote address for a large tech company's annual summit. As always, I shared my story of losing my legs at nineteen and how I'd learned to not only survive but thrive.

The summit's theme was *courage*, so I decided to do something brave and vulnerable: Instead of wrapping up my story with my athletic victories, I decided to share the truth of what I was going through with my current injury. I spoke about the courage it takes to keep moving forward, even when you have no idea what the outcome will be.

"Courage always comes before confidence," I said.

After my talk, a man came up to thank me for sharing my story.

"I used to be in the military," he said. "And your talk reminded me of a saying we had: 'Never get too far from the foxhole.'"

He explained that a foxhole is a four- or five-foot-deep hole in the ground that soldiers use to shield themselves from gunfire and artillery.

"The farther away you get from the foxhole," he warned me, "the more you forget what it was like when you were in it. The more connected you are to the foxhole, the more reminded you are of how precious life is and the more you can help and prepare someone else."

He looked me in the eye. "I think this injury happened to you because you were meant to be brought back to the foxhole. It's here to remind you of what it felt like to be scared, overwhelmed, and uncertain so that you can keep helping others who are still in the thick of it."

My heart began pounding harder. I realized he was right. I had gotten too far from the foxhole—and this injury was calling me back.

Lucky for me, I now had twenty years of hard-won wisdom to draw on. Although my leg injury forced me to relive the pain, fear, and uncertainty I'd experienced when I was nineteen and lost my legs, it also sharpened the memory of all the techniques I'd used to get through those things before.

I started documenting the tools and techniques that helped me in my most difficult moments—strategies I sometimes didn't even realize I was using. As I wrote them down, I began to realize the same practices that helped me survive my darkest days were also the ones that created my greatest days.

I knew that not only would I be able to get through my injury but also I would be living proof that the tools I was using actually work—because I was testing them on myself.

My new injury had brought me close enough to the foxhole that I could once again relate deeply with others who were going through hard times. I wanted to help others—I want to help *you*—bounce forward through the challenges in your own life.

That was when I knew it was time to write this book.

HOW TO USE THIS BOOK

Whereas my first book, *On My Own Two Feet,* was an inspirational memoir of facing the unimaginable and going on to thrive, this book is a toolkit for using adversity to launch yourself into an even better life than the one you'd planned.

Every chapter opens with a story of how I discovered a tool or technique while navigating my leg injury, followed by specific instructions on how to use that tool yourself.

I've done a ton of research on the most up-to-date science behind these tools, and I've spoken and worked with dozens of experts and thought leaders as I've refined them. For two years I recorded a podcast, *Bouncing Forward*, where I interviewed some of the world's top thought leaders, including Amy Cuddy and Elizabeth Gilbert, on resilience, personal growth, and transforming adversity into success, and I've integrated some of my favorite insights from those sessions.

I recommend reading this book from start to finish, as the story is written chronologically—but if you like, you can also go straight to the chapter whose topic feels the most urgent to you on any particular day. If you're short on time, you can even go straight to the "Tool" section at the end of each chapter to start practicing these techniques right away.

ALSO—at the end of this book, you'll find a QR code that unlocks additional Bounce Forward bonus content to support you on your journey.

—

To be clear: This isn't a triumphant comeback story about how I got thrown off course by an injury and then made it back to the top of the mountain. As I type these words, I'm still navigating this new reality and rebuilding myself by using these tools every day. This is a story from the trenches—the middle of the journey, not the end. If you're in the foxhole right now, I'm right there with you.

My hope is that whether or not you can relate to having prosthetic legs, you'll find tools here to help you use your own inevitable setbacks to become an even better, wiser, and more purposeful version of yourself. Like the proverb says, our plans may indeed make God laugh, but the path we end up walking when our plans go awry can be more beautiful than we ever imagined.

Part One

BOUNCE

ONE

GRIEF to *Hope*

IN 2019, I WAS FLYING HIGH.

I had just walked the red carpet at the Golden Globe Awards, where I showcased my polished carbon fiber and titanium legs with three-inch heels and a stunning designer dress with a slit from my ankle to my thigh and represented Paralympians on a glamorous platform. I was being flown to far-flung countries like Spain, Singapore, and China to speak to some of the largest companies in the world.

When I wasn't traveling for speeches or snowboarding, I was working with athletes with disabilities through Adaptive Action Sports, the organization my husband, Daniel, and I had founded in 2005. We had fulfilled our dream of buying and renovating a home in the mountains of Colorado, and I was snowboarding at some of the most beautiful resorts in the world as often as I could. It was heavenly.

Then, in the blink of an eye, I was knocked off my feet. Literally.

On the morning of February 20, I stepped out of my Las Vegas hotel room to deliver a keynote speech to a large real estate company. As I walked down the hallway in my dress, prosthetic legs, and heels, I felt a cramp in my left calf. I paused, thinking, *Maybe I put my leg on wrong?*

I went back to my room and took my leg off. Everything looked fine, so I put it back on. But halfway to the elevator, my calf cramped again.

I had only twenty minutes to get onstage, so I limped to the ballroom.

I usually stand and walk during my speeches, but I felt an enormous amount of pressure in my calf, as if the carbon fiber of my prosthetic was pressing into my muscle. Instead, I stood in one place and leaned on my other leg for the full forty-five minutes, pretending nothing was wrong. The second I stepped offstage, Daniel grabbed a wheelchair and rushed me back to our hotel room.

Once we were there, I took off my prosthetic. My left leg looked unusually pale, nearly white. I thought, *Maybe my prosthetic was too tight? Or maybe I gained water weight from our steak dinner last night? What the heck is going on?*

Just then, I received a text from a friend asking if I was attending the national prosthetic convention that was happening in a hotel just down the street.

"Actually, I'm in Vegas for a speech," I texted back quickly, "but I'm having a prosthetic issue. Maybe someone there can help me!" Daniel and I jumped in a car and headed to the convention.

As soon as we walked in, I tracked down Kevin Carroll, a world-class prosthetist I'd known for years. Carroll is best known for building a prosthetic tail for Winter, the dolphin featured in the movie *Dolphin Tale*. He and a few other prosthetists examined my leg while I explained what I was feeling. We all agreed that everything looked fine, even though it hurt to walk. We decided to experiment by trying a thinner liner (the liner is like a shock-absorbing sock that goes on your leg and adds cushion when wearing a prosthetic), hoping it would create a little more space if the prosthetic was too tight. We also adjusted my leg angles to see if we could relieve pressure on my calf. These changes helped a bit, but not enough. After a few hours, we still couldn't figure out what was causing the pain, so I grabbed a pair of crutches and headed back to the hotel.

The next day I flew to Nebraska to give a speech to a group of farmers. For the first time in twenty years, I went through the airport using a wheelchair and used crutches at the hotel. That evening, I crutched my way onstage and sat on a stool to talk.

The next morning, I jolted awake in excruciating pain.

When I sat up and ripped the covers off, I saw that my entire leg from my thigh down was as white as the sheets I was lying on.

This whole time I had assumed something was wrong with my prosthetic. In that moment, it dawned on me that the problem wasn't my prosthetic—it was *me*.

I swung around and hung my legs off the side of the bed, hoping gravity would get my blood moving. My leg was ice-cold, so I began rubbing it vigorously with one hand, trying to warm it up, while using my other hand to call my manager to book me on the quickest flight home to Denver.

As soon as I landed, a friend picked me up and drove me straight to the ER. The administrator there recognized me from the Paralympics and said, "Miss Purdy, what are you doing here?"

"Maybe I'm crazy," I said, "but I think something is going on with my leg. Right now it seems okay, but this morning it was cold, off-color, hurting, and scaring me."

She escorted me to a room for an ultrasound, then left me alone. I examined my leg and saw that even though the pain had waned, there was now a purple spiderweb-like pattern across my knee and down to the bottom of my leg.

Twenty minutes later, two nurses came sprinting into the room with an IV. "We know what's going on," one said breathlessly. "You have a massive blood clot from your hip down through every artery in your left leg!"

The other said, "This is major. You're lucky you got here when you did. This could cause a stroke."

It felt like déjà vu from twenty years before, when I entered the hospital in septic shock and the nurses were in a state of panic trying to save me.

I began to cry. I called Daniel, who was already rushing down from the mountains, as well as my parents and my manager. "Hurry if you can," I choked out between sobs.

As I was trying to wrap my head around the situation, a nurse I hadn't seen before walked into the room. "We spoke to the surgeons," she said, "and they say there's nothing to worry about. We'll prep your paperwork, and you can leave."

What?

Before I could really protest, she went on. "You're an amputee. Amputees don't have typical blood flow, so this is probably normal for you."

My face got hot, and my heart started racing. Panic bloomed in my chest. I pleaded, "Please listen. I've never had a blood clot in my leg before. I promise you, this isn't normal!"

She said, "Guaranteed, most amputees have blood clots in their legs and don't even know it."

"Sure," I said, "but most amputees with blood clots are older than me and have underlying conditions like vascular disease or diabetes. That's usually why they lost a limb in the first place! My situation is different. I'm an athlete who snowboards for six hours a day. This is not normal for me. I know for a fact that I've never had a blood clot in my leg before, and I've never felt anything like this."

I took a deep breath. "I *know* my body," I said. "I know something major is happening to my leg. I'm not leaving the hospital until I speak to a surgeon."

Luckily, the nurse relented and admitted me to a room. Daniel arrived, and I spent the night in the hospital so that I could speak with the vascular surgeons in the morning.

The next day, two surgeons walked into my room. One of them was a young, good-looking guy, who, according to the morning nurse, was "a new hotshot everyone's been talking about." But I wasn't impressed. He had the same dismissive attitude as the nurse from the day before.

"Unfortunately, because you're an amputee, you're already the worst-case scenario," he said. "Within two weeks, the clot in your leg will harden, and your leg will be inoperable. It will harden like a cement pipe—permanently. People like you have to learn how to live with things like this."

Excuse me?

I thought, *This guy has no clue who I am, what my situation is, or what I was capable of before I came in here. I can't believe I have to plead with these doctors to even consider the possibility that a massive blood clot in my leg isn't normal.*

I realized that they were used to textbook amputees. They didn't see me as an individual. Instead, they were lumping me into a category where I didn't fit.

In panic and tears, I pleaded with the surgeons. "I'm not like other amputees you've seen," I said. "I'm a professional athlete—a three-time Paralympic medalist. I've spent the past twenty years training and competing intensely with no issues, not to mention traveling the world and standing on stages for sixty minutes at a time delivering talks, all with zero pain. Please understand, my situation is different."

Daniel took out his phone and pulled up images of me snowboarding and dancing on *Dancing with the Stars.* "Look at what Amy can do on her legs!" he urged them. "This isn't normal for her. Please. There has to be something you can do."

I questioned them about specific treatment options, but they dismissed each one. When I asked about bypass surgery to bring blood to my lower leg, they said it was impossible "because you don't have an ankle or a foot to bypass the blood to." They rattled off all the options a person with a "normal" leg would have—then explained why none of those options would work for me. According to them, I would just have to learn to deal with the pain and the slower pace of life, and if things got bad enough, I would have no choice but to amputate my leg higher up.

In that moment, I realized doctors have the power to give you hope or strip it away. Right then, they stripped every bit of hope I had that I would be comfortable in my legs again.

I stared at them in disbelief. "I can't get my prosthetic on," I said. "I can't even walk! My leg is ice-cold, in pain, and clearly not a healthy color. And you're going to send me home to live like this?"

The hotshot surgeon said, "Maybe someday you'll be able to wear your leg again and walk to the mailbox and back. That's what we tell most amputees with vascular disease—to start small."

Are you kidding me? I thought. *First of all, I don't have vascular disease. Second, are you telling me I'm going to go from being a professional athlete to barely being able to walk to the mailbox and back? That's it? That's my prognosis?*

I was trying so hard to get them to see me as *me*, not just as a statistic.

As they turned toward the door to leave, I literally yelled, "Please, *see me!*"

I asked one more time: "Nothing can be done? Nothing at all?"

My whole life, I've lived by the philosophy that everything can be figured out one way or another. How could it be that there was simply no treatment available for me? Could twenty years of living an extraordinary life and performing on my legs at the highest level really vanish in a matter of minutes?

Grief and loss swept over me. The hopelessness I felt was like a huge dark hole in my chest. It was total devastation, like nothing I had ever felt before.

The surgeons must have realized I was finished advocating for myself, because they walked out of the room. I then cried harder than I ever have in my life. I wailed from the depths of my soul—hard enough that you could hear me down the hallway. Daniel was there to witness it all. This was my worst, and he was in it with me.

Nothing can prepare you for loss. Nothing can prepare you for grief. Whether you know the loss is coming or not, it hits you like a tsunami and slams you into the depths of despair.

If you haven't yet experienced grief or loss, you will. The longer we live, the more time we have to become attached to our lives and what's in them, and the more likely it is that we will lose something or someone we love. Grief is as human as human gets, and it is one of the most painful feelings we can experience.

As I sobbed in that room at the hospital, I was grieving the loss of my life as I knew it: my abilities, my purpose, and the identity I had built around rebounding from a major setback to become a strong, successful athlete and speaker.

Who am I now? I wondered. I had no idea. My success story had been such a big part of my identity for the past twenty years. Who would I be if I could no longer do the things that made me who I was?

Believe it or not, the loss I felt in that moment was even worse than when I lost both of my legs below the knees in the first place. The difference was that this time I wasn't fighting a battle between life and death. I was fighting for the *quality* of my life, which somehow felt even more painful.

—

That afternoon, I had one more conversation with the surgeons. After I pleaded for hours, they finally agreed to "try something." The following morning, they made an incision into my groin and removed the blood clot from my femoral artery, though they weren't able to remove it below the knee.

My mom flew in to be with me, and we left the hospital three days later. Normally after a surgery, you get to walk away knowing the issue is "fixed." But when my mom and I left the hospital, I knew this journey wasn't over; it was only just beginning.

We checked into a hotel right next door to the hospital. Knowing my leg had little blood flow from the knee down, I didn't feel confident going back up to our home in the mountains. I spent most of the next few days lying in bed recovering. Waves of grief continued to crash into me at the most unexpected moments. Sometimes it felt like I could barely come up for air, and I found myself gasping for breath as I sobbed.

Grief can feel like getting caught in an ocean wave. Some waves slam into you hard and fast. Others are slow-moving, and you can feel them building before they crest. But no matter how hard you try to avoid a wave or how fast you swim to get to shore, that wave is going to pull you in and pummel you just the same.

They say that if you get sucked into the undertow, fighting it will only exhaust you. Instead, the best thing to do is relax, knowing the wave will release you.

That's how grief works too.

Even though I had experienced grief before, this time was different. It felt as if everything I'd worked for since losing my legs was being ripped away from me in an instant.

I started flashing back to what it was like after I contracted meningitis. Believe it or not, the hardest part wasn't losing my legs—it was the idea that thanks to the kidney failure, I was losing my health. I stayed on dialysis for a year and a half, going to every doctor imaginable in the hopes of finding a magic cure for my kidneys.

I remember the day I lost all hope that my kidneys would heal. A well-known nephrologist came to our home to go over test results. As I sat in my wheelchair at our dining room table, I remember him telling us there was nothing more that could be done. "You're in full kidney failure," he declared. "Your only hope is to stay on dialysis, which isn't a good way to live, or have a kidney transplant."

After he left, I went back to my bedroom, fell out of my wheelchair onto my knees on the floor, and pleaded with God or whoever holds the power to *please please please make my kidneys come back.* I cried and pleaded until I ran out of tears.

The loss, fear, and pain I felt in that moment felt like too much to bear. And yet somehow, little by little, I picked myself up and moved forward. I eventually received a transplant from my dad and went on to live a full, healthy life.

Remembering how my greatest fear had turned into my biggest miracle gave me the smallest sliver of hope that maybe I could do it again. Maybe even with the injury and the horrible prognosis from the surgeons, I would be okay. *Maybe the worst-case scenario isn't that bad after all*, I thought.

When I grieved my kidneys at age twenty-one, I learned the power of allowing grief to flow through me rather than fighting it. Falling to my knees and pleading felt horrible, but it was a necessary step in my process. When you let grief in, it moves *through* you, which is exactly what needs to happen for you to process it. After the wave passes, you feel a little more like yourself. You can raise your head above water. And usually, once all the tears have dried up, a little ray of hope begins to shine through.

During those early stages of mourning, I started retreating to my bathtub whenever I needed to grieve and process my emotions. Even today, I use the quiet time submerged in hot water as a refuge. In the bath, I can cry as long and hard as I need to, knowing I'm in a safe space to feel whatever needs to be felt.

In the hotel room where I was staying with my mom, I couldn't take baths because of the surgery and the large incision in my thigh. But I did find comfort in a warm shower. I would sit on the floor with the hot water pouring over me and cry until I ran out of tears. I'd go in there feeling like the world was ending and emerge with a clearer head and a smidgen of hope that maybe this wasn't the end of the world after all.

I didn't step out of the shower feeling *good*—grief is brutal by any definition. But by letting my pain flow through me, I felt a little lighter and clearer, and that was enough.

Healing doesn't happen overnight or on any kind of predictable schedule. Grieving can take a long time and often involves a lot of work. But allowing grief in instead of fighting it eases the process. Taking those showers helped me move forward even though I continued to feel shrouded in darkness, fear, and pain.

Later, I learned about the biochemistry behind this phenomenon. Going through a major loss throws our body chemistry out of balance. Levels of feel-good neurotransmitters like serotonin, dopamine, and oxytocin plummet while levels of stress hormones rise. This imbalance feels terrible, and it's not just an emotion but a true physical ache. We call it *heart*break for a reason.

But when we let grief flow through us, our chemistry resets a bit. The body turns off the stress response and triggers the release of feel-good endorphins and oxytocin; we shift from an activated sympathetic nervous system state to a calmer parasympathetic one.

This explains why I was able to find a hint of hope after the showers where I poured out my fears, tears, and grief.

When the doctors took all hope away from me, I found it again through the grieving process itself. Sitting in that hotel room, I couldn't see a path to thriving. But my shred of hope helped me survive.

You might not feel amazing after a huge cry, but you'll probably feel at least a little more peace, calm, and levelheadedness. The relief you feel might be tiny, but this is where you can find your hope.

Riding the wave of grief is what let me survive one day, then the next, and the next. And it can help you too. When you surrender to the waves instead of struggling against them, you realize they're not just trying to drag you under—they're slowly and steadily pushing you back to shore.

TOOL: RIDE THE WAVE OF GRIEF

Grief is one of the most powerful emotions we can feel, yet most of the time, we're lost at sea when it comes to dealing with it. Whether you're mourning the loss of a loved one, a relationship, or a dream that didn't come true, grieving fully will help you find hope. Here are the four key lessons I've learned for processing grief:

1. Let yourself feel it.

Often, our instinct is to avoid pain and heartache. We suppress negative emotions or distract ourselves from them because we think this will keep us safe. But you will never actually heal your pain unless you give yourself time and space to feel, process, and grieve. The expression "You have to feel it to heal it" speaks to the truth of this phenomenon.

Grief is there for a reason. It's a sign you really cared about something. And the more you love something, the harder it is to let it go. Grief cracks your heart wide open. Letting yourself feel the pain of loss is what gives you the full experience of love.

Let your grief in, and it will move through and out of you, often taking the negative feelings with it. Don't avoid grief. Welcome it as a part of your healing journey. The more you feel, the more you will heal.

2. Create a safe space for grief to flow.

Find a place where you can let your grief flow with zero judgment. This might be a private space like a bathtub or shower, your bedroom, or a spot in nature where you can be alone or it might be in the company of a therapist, friend, or loved one who has the capacity to support you and who you feel comfortable crying around.

Often, we try to hide or minimize our grief out of fear of overwhelming others, and this can cause all those painful emotions to get trapped inside us.

When you're in your safe space or with your safe person, let yourself cry and process as much as you need to, without worrying about what it looks or sounds like. Don't try to edit your grief or force it into a certain shape or size. Just let it flow.

3. Schedule time to grieve.

Most of us can't spend entire days grieving. We have to work, take care of kids, or manage to-do lists. We need to keep going, whether or not we feel ready or even able.

If at all possible, designate a specific time and place for grieving. When you feel grief building up, go to your safe space. If you have to hold it in for a while until you can get to your safe space, that's okay. Do that. But once you get there, let it all out.

As hard as it may be, allow yourself to really feel the full force of the storm during the time you've scheduled.

4. Look for the thread of hope.

Notice how you feel after a wave of grief hits. If you really let it flow, you'll often find yourself a little calmer and more clearheaded.

Look for your thread of hope and hold on to it. This might be a specific thought like *I will love again* or *I will beat this diagnosis*, or it might be a general statement like *One way or another, it will be okay.*

If you lose your thread of hope (and you will!), know that you can find it again after the next wave. Allow yourself to entertain the possibility that even though this feels like the end of the world, maybe it's not.

—

Grief isn't something to get over—it's a wave to ride, your heart's way of honoring all you've loved and lost. The waves will keep coming, but with every one you ride, you're building your capacity to handle whatever life brings next. What might feel like drowning one moment is actually your soul learning to swim in deeper waters, giving you a full experience of your own humanity.

TWO

HELPLESS to *Empowered*

DURING THOSE DAYS in the hotel room, my leg was ice-cold, painful, and purple. My mind was flooded with fear, uncertainty, and deep sadness that this reality was now my life.

I had a huge incision in my groin from where the doctors had cut into me to remove the clot from my femoral artery. The physical pain in my leg constantly reminded me that something was wrong. I'd had surgery, yet nothing was fixed. I alternated between moments of paralyzing sadness and moments of urgent activity because I knew if I didn't *do something*, I might never walk in my prosthetic leg again.

The surgeons' bone-chilling prognosis that the blood clot in my arteries would harden and become inoperable within two weeks was never far from my mind. I spent most of my time in that hotel room frantically researching on my laptop or making phone call after phone call, trying to learn everything I could about my situation. I still didn't know what had caused the injury in the first place. But because the doctors had released me without giving me instructions for next steps, I had to figure it out on my own. If I didn't, I might never walk again.

Two weeks is a very short amount of time in which to investigate a mysterious injury, find experts who can help you, and convince them to schedule and perform surgery on you.

I wondered, *Am I in a nightmare?* That's certainly how it felt.

I reached out to everyone I knew who might have an in with the best vascular doctors and surgeons in the country. One of these people was Oprah Winfrey. Another was Dr. Oz, whom I'd met while speaking at a conference a few years before. Dr. Oz got me in touch with a doctor at the Cleveland Clinic.

Meanwhile, my mom faxed my medical documents to doctors around the country, asking, *Can anything be done?* We continued to get the same answer: No. The explanation was always the same: "You are already an amputee. Your arteries are so small, they'll only close up again. The two-week window is too short to do something effective."

These responses sent me into a panic—but they also motivated me. I refused to give up on myself. What if these doctors were wrong?

Lucky for me, I had a *lot* of practice knocking down doors. When I first lost my legs twenty years before, I knew that all I wanted to do was snowboard again. At the time, all the doctors and prosthetists said snowboarding with two prosthetic legs was most likely impossible. They didn't know of any prosthetic feet designed for snowboarding. "This is the best it will get and feel," they'd say.

Back then, I had to search high and low for help. I cold-called adaptive ski organizations across the country and prosthetic manufacturers around the world. I sent handwritten letters. It took me a whole year of trying until I found just *one* person with experience snowboarding with a prosthetic leg, who then put me in touch with *one* company that could help me. In the meantime, I spent hours researching and experimenting to design my own snowboarding feet.

Now, in this hotel room, aching physically and emotionally, I had to fight even harder. The doctors I spoke with already saw me as a worst-case scenario. And I was under this intense time limit. Nevertheless, I refused to accept that the long period of thriving with my legs had come to an end.

In the past, it always seemed like I'd meet just the right person at just the right time to give me the solutions I needed. I thought of those people as my angels.

Where were my angels now?

One night in the middle of that two-week window, I finally found one—and in an unexpected place. At about 11:00 p.m., my leg began throbbing worse than before. My mom and I went across the parking lot to the ER to see if they could do an ultrasound to assess if something had changed since my surgery.

After the ultrasound, a very kind ER doctor said, "Honey, I'm really concerned about your knee. You have little to no blood flow. You need to get back to your surgeon ASAP to see how he can help."

My first thought was, *Ugh, go back to the guy who said there was nothing more he could do?* But as desperate as I was, I called his office the next morning just in case he'd had a sudden change of heart and learned that he was out of town for the week. "I don't have a week to spare!" I told the office assistant. "I have to see someone now!" They offered to get me in with another surgeon, Dr. Cooper, who was available at 4:00 p.m. that day.

"Yes! I'll take it!" I said.

Dr. Cooper was a warm and gentle older man. When he walked into the examination room, he said, "Your previous surgeon gave me his notes saying there is nothing that can be done about your leg."

My heart sank. I started pleading and telling him who I was and what I had accomplished. "I need help," I said. "Now. Please."

I was surprised to hear him gently reply, "Okay, let's take a look."

He took me into the ultrasound room for a scan. During the scan, he raised his eyebrows and said, "Whoa. This is serious. You have only a small spiderweb of blood feeding blood to your knee and lower leg." He made intentional eye contact first with my mom, then with me, and said, "Typically, with an amputee in this situation, I wouldn't do anything because I don't think I could help. But you remind me of my daughter. If she were in this situation, I would do everything in my power to help her. I'd like to schedule surgery this week to see what we can do."

I couldn't believe it. *Yes!* With a twinkle in his eye, he said, "You know, unlike these younger hotshot surgeons, I've been doing this for twenty-five years. I have a few tools in my toolbox that those guys don't. Let's get in there and see what we can do."

Four days later, I headed into surgery with a glimmer of hope that he could help my leg.

The first thing the nurse said to me when I woke up from that surgery was that she'd never seen Dr. Cooper work so long or so hard on someone. "Normally he's in there for two hours, but he was in there for four, and he gave it everything he had," she said.

Dr. Cooper came in and explained that he had diligently cleared out every blood vessel he could find behind and below my knee. He'd then put in a catheter to drip tPA (tissue plasminogen activator), a major blood clot dissolver, into my arteries. He said it would remain there until they ran clear.

I was in a lot of pain, but I still felt an avalanche of relief. *Wow. Thank God. I finally found an angel to help me.* I didn't know what the outcome would be, and neither did he, but the simple fact that I wasn't alone and that we had tried something gave me a sliver of hope. *Maybe I can wear my prosthetic and walk again*, I thought.

It wasn't lost on me that to arrive at this hard-won moment of optimism, I'd had to make the first move. In fact, I'd made about a hundred moves in those two weeks leading up to the surgery. It was only after I'd knocked on every door and spoken with every surgeon that I'd found Dr. Cooper.

I was learning the same crucial lesson all over again: Nobody will ever care about you, your body, or your life as much as you do. Nobody is going to save you. You have to save yourself. You need to be your own biggest advocate. You need to fight for your life and your quality of life.

This is how you become a victor instead of a victim.

I've spoken on many panels about self-advocacy, where I've met many medical professionals who've seen firsthand how patients who advocate for themselves secure better outcomes. The research on self-advocacy backs up these observations. For example, in a study of people getting help with mental illness,[1] those who advocated for themselves had more hope, better quality of life, and fewer symptoms than those who did not.

I've also read compelling research on the importance of self-advocacy in other domains of life, like business and finances. One common area in which it really helps is negotiating for a higher salary. According to Fidelity Investments,[2] 58 percent of young professionals do not negotiate their job offers; however, 87 percent of those who do increase their starting salaries by an average of $5,000.

When you advocate for yourself, you increase your likelihood of meeting the people who can help you reach your goals—whatever those goals may be. If you talk to only one or two doctors or other professionals, you get only a small number of ideas and opinions. But when you reach out to dozens or even hundreds of people, you dramatically expand the bank of expertise you're drawing on, and this makes it more likely that you will find the information you need.

In my situation, I knew there had to be *somebody* out there willing to help me. And I wasn't willing to give up until I found that support.

Of course, I want to acknowledge the role of privilege in securing access to help and resources. I know that I have unique privileges when I advocate for myself. Some of this privilege is structural, since I'm a white woman with a public-facing career. And some of it has been earned through hard work and sheer persistence.

Socioeconomic differences are very real, and factors like financial stress and lack of access to health care can be huge barriers when reaching out for the support you need. Unfortunately, systemic injustices make it even more imperative to be your own advocate.

But no matter what your situation looks like, advocating for yourself will almost always get you better results than passively accepting whatever advice or treatment you happen to receive. The important thing is to find the people who will hear you and help you, even if it takes persistence to get there. Know your worth and what you want for your life. Knock down doors until you find the angels and resources you need. If you look hard enough, you will always find them.

Remember, just because the solution you're looking for doesn't exist right now, that doesn't mean it won't in the future. Technology is always advancing. Many times when I've gotten together with experts like surgeons or prosthetists, we've explored new possibilities for health and movement that hadn't existed yet. For example, we created a new foot design suitable for snowboarding. That only happened because I knocked down doors to find the team that could help me.

Some people find all this self-reliance a little scary. They want to latch on to the first authoritative voice and don't bother searching for second opinions. But when you do that, you leave options on the table. Casting a wide net is a *good* thing, and more often than not, it yields better results than simply accepting the first thing you hear.

Whether it's your physical, mental, or spiritual health, a job, a goal, or a dream, you have to value your life enough to save it yourself. When you fight for yourself, you will eventually find others who will fight for you too.

TOOL: BE YOUR OWN BIGGEST ADVOCATE

Being a good advocate for yourself doesn't always come naturally, but it's a skill you can improve with practice. Many of us were raised to be polite and deferential, especially when dealing with experts like doctors, but sometimes a little persistence is warranted, especially when your well-being is on the line. Here are seven steps to becoming your own biggest advocate:

1. Believe you are worthy.

First and foremost, you need to value your life enough to fight for it. You need to believe that you are worthy of the best life possible and refuse to settle for a diminished quality of life, even if doing so would be more convenient for the experts responsible for your care.

2. Set goals.

Be specific. Know what you are looking for. You may wish to give yourself time frames or deadlines for finding answers if that helps motivate you.

3. Research.

The more educated you are about your goals, health, finances, or whatever it may be, the less you will be forced to rely on someone else's opinions to guide you.

For example, most medical staff aren't prepared for someone like me. I show up with knowledge, questions, and research. I'm prepared to tell them much more about my own body than they can tell me while also being open to new ideas and information.

Pick up the phone. Google. Read. Call doctors, companies, and people in the know. Ask them questions. Then ask more. When you are well informed, you are less likely to get railroaded into agreeing to a plan that doesn't serve your needs.

4. Form relationships with people whose values align with your own.

Unlike the first surgeons who examined me, Dr. Cooper was willing to take risks. As a risk-taker myself, he was exactly the kind of person I needed. My kidney transplant doctor is another example. He knows that I love to travel and live a full life with my transplant. Unlike other transplant doctors who are overly cautious about travel, we worked together to create a plan that allows me to live the life I want. With his help, I was even on *The Amazing Race*, where I raced and traveled all over the world.

Start building a team of people who value the same things you do. They will help you find creative solutions instead of falling back on "it can't be done." Ultimately, they will advocate alongside you, and their support will strengthen your position immeasurably.

5. Be assertive.

Practice speaking up for your goals, dreams, and values. Assertiveness doesn't mean being angry or rude. It means knowing your rights and your worth and speaking up for them.

Often, assertiveness boils down to having a clear yes and no. *Yes, I need to get this treatment. No, I won't agree to that plan.*

When you practice assertiveness, you'll find that you become clearer and more confident in your interactions with others, as you are no longer trying to suppress your true desires, needs, or feelings. This paves the way to getting what you really want, not what others think you should have.

6. Be persistent.

When you advocate for yourself, there are moments when you will experience resistance. Don't let discouragement defeat you. Keep knocking down doors until there are no more doors to knock down.

When you look for advice, try to consult multiple experts. After all, even experts have limits to their training and experience. When they say no to you, it's a no according to their own ability and willingness to explore what else is possible, not a final no from the whole universe.

7. Be kind.

While advocating for yourself, always be kind to the person you're talking to. Kindness makes people want to help you. Being kind opens more doors in life than almost anything else. You want people to *want* to open their doors to you.

If you can meet with the people you're consulting in person, that can take you much further than using only phone or email. Face-to-face interactions give you a chance to demonstrate your humanity and for the kindness in your heart to shine through.

—

Nobody will ever care about your health as much as you do. When you become your own biggest advocate, you stop waiting for someone to save you and start taking your destiny into your own hands. The world is full of people who can help you—but none of them can help if they don't know you exist. Your persistence, your research, and your refusal to take no for an answer can mean the difference between settling for a dismal outcome and finding the solution you need.

THREE

ANXIOUS to *Calm*

WHEN I WOKE UP FROM THE SURGERY Dr. Cooper performed on me, I was in more pain than I'd ever experienced in my life.

Doctors often ask patients to rate their pain on a scale from one to ten. After the surgery, my pain was off the charts. It felt like acid was being pumped into my arteries, which was basically *true* because the tPA clot-busting solution was dripping in from a catheter and would continue until my arteries were clear and blood could flow freely. Not even dose after dose of fentanyl could take the edge off the pain of the tPA. With Daniel and my mom by my side, I moaned and whimpered for hours.

I stayed in this level of pain for two solid days until the tPA finished its work and my arteries cleared. Finally, the catheter was removed, the burning pain subsided, and the medical team discharged me. Dr. Cooper had saved my leg—for now. But the journey was still only just beginning.

Going home after your entire life has been flipped upside down and inside out is surreal. When my mom and I checked out of the hotel and headed to my house in the mountains, I felt just like I had when I went home after losing my legs in the first place. Everything looked the same, yet everything had changed. Standing on one leg in my entryway for the first time since this ordeal began, I knew I had entered uncharted territory.

Years ago, when Daniel and I were shopping for a house, I had decided that because I like exercise, we should have a three-story home. I figured we could always move into a single-story house when we were much older, but that would be decades down the road.

I never imagined that I would be knocked off my feet at this point in my life. So here I was with one good leg (my right prosthetic leg) and three sets of stairs to climb. Daniel, my mom, and I decided the best thing to do was to set me up on the couch downstairs. We'd make a new living space for me on the main floor so that I wouldn't have to scoot up to our bedroom, which was (of course!) on the top floor.

For a long time, all I could do was sit on the couch. I couldn't move around the house comfortably, cook, do ordinary tasks for myself, or even get upright without assistance. It was maddening. I've always relied on physical movement to support my mental health, and I was a stickler about cleaning. Now all I could do was sit and look at the dust on the floor, knowing I couldn't do anything about it.

And then there was the pain.

Although Dr. Cooper had succeeded at clearing out my arteries, my leg was far from healthy. The tPA had inflamed every vessel and capillary in my leg, and it was swollen to three times its normal size. It would go from white to purple, even to blue at times. After weeks of enduring this nonstop, I realized this was what chronic pain felt like.

Just before this injury happened, someone on Instagram had reached out to me and said, "Amy, I love everything you share about resilience, but what do you do if you're suffering from chronic pain that seems like it will never get better?"

At the time, I hadn't known how to respond. Many people assume that having prosthetic legs hurts, but that's not always the case. My legs had *never* really hurt unless I stood on them for too long or landed flat off a big jump while snowboarding. But this new, relentless pain was torturous.

Pain forces you into your body. You can't escape it. It becomes impossible to think about anything else, impossible to get inspired or excited for the future. I had always been so motivated and excited about life. But in this pain, I couldn't even remember what that felt like. The physical pain, the uncertain prognosis, the isolation, and the months trapped on my couch—all combined with the fear I would never recover—threw me into an anxiety-ridden tailspin.

Nighttime was the worst. Daniel and I would be watching a movie when suddenly my chest would tighten up, my breathing would get shallow, and I would start gasping for air, my heart skipping beats. I would feel my lungs squeeze as the weight of the world crushed in on me.

It became a pattern: try to relax and watch a movie, spiral into panic. Before the injury, Daniel and I used to set aside evenings to relax and connect. But ever since I'd gotten home from my last surgery, I would feel myself going mad the moment the sun began to dip.

In those moments, Daniel saw the worst of me. I would become consumed by what-if questions: *What if I never walk again? What if I can't snowboard again? What if I can't even walk onstage again? What if all the magical divine interventions I remembered in the past weren't as real as I believed them to be? What if God and the divine aren't real, and I actually just have really bad luck and my quality of life will never be the same?*

And then there were the why-me questions: *Why do I have to go through something so tragic and traumatic, AGAIN? Why are there people in the world who glide through life in perfect health and don't lose a limb along the way? I have helped so many people in my life! We built a whole organization around it. I have literally inspired millions around the world. What did I do wrong to deserve this? Didn't I learn all the lessons I was supposed to learn the first time? Didn't I make lemonade out of lemons in every way possible? Why me? Why AGAIN?*

I would cry and rant until I'd nearly scared my husband off, then scoot up the stairs on my butt and get into the bathtub to yell at God.

My mom lived with us for a few months, cooking and taking care of both Daniel and me. One night we were flipping through Netflix.

"Let's watch this documentary," she said. It was called *Be Here Now.*[3]

Not knowing anything about it, we turned it on. I braced myself for the flood of anxiety that had become my new normal. But this time, nothing happened.

Be Here Now tells the story of actor Andy Whitfield and his wife, Vashti, after he receives a terminal non-Hodgkin's lymphoma diagnosis while starring in the popular series *Spartacus: Blood and Sand.* The film documents Whitfield and Vashti traveling the world seeking doctors, spiritual healers, and any possible advice or help. No matter how out of the box a potential solution was, Whitfield tried it. He sought a cure with relentless dedication. Tragically, he ultimately succumbed to the cancer.

The aspect of Whitfield's story I found most striking was how he discovered the best healer of all to be the present moment. He had a mantra he repeated whenever he began spiraling into anxiety: "Be here now." Whitfield said it reminded him to be present and to enjoy the moments he had left.

That night, sitting on the couch, I grabbed a sticky note off the side table, wrote "be here now," and put it in my wallet so that I'd see it as often as possible and have it handy whenever I got anxious. From then on, that simple phrase helped me refocus my thoughts and see that my anxiety was the fear of the future—but in the present moment, I was okay.

Anxiety happens when we're afraid of what might come next, but it dissolves when we're fully present. In fact, it's impossible to be present and anxious at the same time. You're either in the moment where you are alive and well or you are mentally in the future with all of your fears and uncertainties. You can't be in both places at the same time.

When the brain detects a potential threat, including an uncertain future, it turns on the stress response, putting the sympathetic nervous system into overdrive. Our pupils dilate to take in more information, our muscles tense, our breath shortens, our heart races, and our thoughts start going a mile a minute—all to help us prepare to survive in the face of a threat. This happens whether the threat is there with us in the moment or if it's something we fear happening soon.

This might have been useful back in the time when humans often had to fight off lions and other major physical threats. But it's really disruptive when we're stuck on the couch feeling anxious.

Fortunately, humans have the ability to calm this whole thing down. When we practice grounding ourselves in the present moment, we release our panicked thoughts about the future. When you pay attention to where you are—the physical sensations, the sights and sounds—your body starts to understand that in this moment, you are safe.

As I sat on the couch and reminded myself to *be here now*, I reeled my mind back in from where it had wandered off into the future and reminded myself that all of those things I was so worried about weren't actually happening.

I realized I'd been using present moment grounding techniques for decades. As a professional athlete, there were plenty of moments when my sympathetic nervous system was activated—like standing in the start gates of a Paralympic race or in the wings about to walk onstage to deliver a keynote address. In moments like those, things like pupil dilation and heightened alertness can actually be helpful.

Instead of letting the uncomfortable aspects of this activation distract me, I focused on the ways my nervous system was serving me. I found a way to be in that heightened state *and* deeply at peace at the same time, free of the panic, anxiety, and fear that so often go along with a racing heart and sweaty palms.

—

Psychologists have identified a mental state called flow, which is characterized by a heightened sense of presence and focused awareness. Flow states happen when you are so immersed in the present moment that the world and all distractions seem to fall away. You're so absorbed in what you're doing that you don't even think; instead, you feel a sense of timelessness and effortlessness. This is true whether you're doing an everyday task like washing your hair or a high-powered, demanding activity like careening down a mountain at sixty mph. Flow is pure, immersive presence at the highest level. To me, it's the fullest, most amplified way of being in the present moment.

The first time I experienced a flow state was in 2014 on *Dancing with the Stars*. When I first started the show, I would get so nervous when I went onstage that I would almost black out the whole performance. When it was over, I would have a moment of coming to, thinking, *I don't even know what happened out there!*

Dancing (or doing anything) with that level of anxiety never really feels good. You tend to get ahead of the music or behind it and are always at least a little out of sync. My goal by the end of the eleven weeks was to feel like I was right in the pocket of the music when I danced: not a millisecond too fast or too slow. Finally, in week nine, the week of the Argentine tango, I nailed it: I was in the pocket.

As I danced on what I like to call my tippy-toe feet—they were swimming feet I'd transformed into dancing feet so that I could rise *en pointe* like a ballerina—I slipped into a state of pure presence. I could see the expressions on each face in the audience as if time was standing still. Unlike my previous dances that passed in a blur, I had total clarity. I moved with the music, yet somehow the world around me had completely slowed down. In that moment, I achieved my goal: a state of presence so vivid, I'll never forget it.

After experiencing that first flow state, my goal became to find the same experience when I snowboarded. I used the mental practice of present moment awareness in every race leading up to the 2018 Paralympic Games, where I ultimately won bronze and silver medals.

When you are completely present in the here and now, the world fades away, and you realize just how much time and mental bandwidth you actually have to make decisions. Science has shown that when you are in a flow state, your brain reduces activity in regions associated with self-consciousness and thinking about the future. This frees you up to become more creative and to find the solutions you need at the right time. A flow state doesn't just make you perform at your best; it allows you to think your clearest. It's so cool!

You don't need to be an athlete to experience flow and its benefits. It's something we can all practice. Present moment awareness can help with preparing a sales meeting, giving a talk, or even writing a book. Artists often describe experiencing flow when they paint, draw, or dance: They lock into the moment, and it's as if time stops and the world falls away. Their expression *flows.*

These days, I always remind myself before going onstage to speak or doing a public interview that even though I may be a little nervous about it, as long as I am present, I will always make the right decisions in the moment.

And you can too.

Be present in the moment, and not only will you stop anxiety in its tracks but you will also learn to enjoy the little details of life—and you'll be able to perform at your best when you need to. When you focus completely on the task at hand, the pressure of the world falls away and you realize that you are okay, right here, right now.

TOOL: PRACTICE PRESENCE

Although it may seem like calm people were just born that way, the truth is that most people who can stop an anxiety spiral in its tracks became adept through practice. Here are two techniques you can use both in high-stakes moments and in everyday situations when your anxiety is spiking:

1. Repeat the Be Here Now mantra.

When you notice anxiety brewing, take a deep breath and focus on one thing in front of you: a leaf outside the window, a piece of furniture, or the painting on the wall. Study every little detail: its color, texture, and shape, whether it's wet or dry, smooth or scratchy. Let yourself become completely absorbed in this object.

Next, silently speak the words *be here now.*

As you repeat this mantra, slow your breathing and focus on what's happening right here, right now. Continue repeating the mantra until you feel calm. Remember: No matter what happens later, you're okay right now because you're here, and you're alive. You'll meet those future moments as they come.

2. Try the Still Lake meditation.

During the 2018 Paralympic Games, I used a meditation and breathing technique called the Still Lake meditation to calm myself. Here's how it works:

- When you are feeling anxious or worrying about the future, close your eyes.
- Take a deep breath that fills your lungs to their fullest capacity.
- With your eyes still closed and while holding your breath, imagine you are looking at a lake with ripples spreading over it, as if you just threw a pebble into the water.
- Now let your breath out slowly and imagine the ripples calming down and widening.
- Recognize that it's your slow and controlled exhale that is calming the water.
- Continue to exhale until all your breath is gone, your lungs are empty, and the water is perfectly still.

—

If it often feels like anxiety takes the reins and you have no control, don't despair. With gentle, persistent effort, you can change the way your mind responds in moments of stress or pressure: no longer racing into the future but staying right where you are. By homing in on the tiny details, you not only alleviate anxiety but also tap into the beauty that is always around you while freeing your mind and body to perform their best.

If you'd like to be guided through this practice,
scan the QR code at the end of the book,
which will take you to resources
that will walk you through it step-by-step.

FOUR

OVERWHELMED to *Composed*

WHEN IT RAINS, IT POURS.

As if everything I was dealing with wasn't enough, I started having new health crises shortly after returning home to Colorado.

First came the bleeding. Now that my femoral and popliteal arteries were open, we needed to keep them that way. This required a hefty dose of blood thinners, which have side effects of their own. For me, the worst side effect was that once my monthly period started, it didn't stop. (For any guys who are reading this, sorry if this is TMI!). I bled so much, for so long, I was certain I had no blood left in my body. For a month straight, Daniel made daily runs to the store and came back with bags of extra absorbent pads flung over his shoulder—definitely not what he thought he was signing up for when he married me. Luckily, he took it all in stride and would joke about how he would hide them in his grocery cart while he was at the store. Either way, thanks, honey!

It took six weeks to get in to see my doctor, who told me that as long as I was on a blood thinner, I may never stop bleeding. The only option was another surgery. I went in for that immediately.

While I was at the OB/GYN, I decided to get my annual mammogram just to check it off my to-do list. For the first time ever, it came back abnormal. I needed follow-up scans at a different hospital in Denver to screen for malignancy. Within the same time frame, I also found out I had a nodule on my thyroid that needed a biopsy to screen for malignancy—at another hospital in Denver. That month I was in three different hospitals, had two different procedures, and was waiting on test results to make sure I didn't have two kinds of cancer.

Throughout all this, we had major scares about my leg too. Several times I woke up in the middle of the night with serious pain. Concerned that my leg wasn't getting enough blood, we'd rush to the ER in Denver, a full ninety-minute drive from our home.

Between the surgeries, the abnormal scan results, and the ongoing trouble with my leg, one thing was becoming clear to me: The world was trying to kill me.

I kept thinking, *What did I do to deserve this? Is my time on this earth over? Is the universe telling me it's my time to go?*

I said to Daniel, "I've lost my light. It's dimmed down to the barest flicker. I feel like I'm barely surviving."

To say I felt overwhelmed would be a massive understatement.

But lucky for me, I was no stranger to overwhelm. In fact, I'd gotten very familiar with it twenty years earlier.

When I first lost my legs, there were days that felt like a never-ending gauntlet of fear and stress. I'd go straight from an emotionally exhausting prosthetic appointment to a lab where technicians would draw vials of blood to see if my kidneys had improved, then to yet another appointment where I'd learn I needed a hearing aid too. Sometimes I was so exhausted that when I wasn't sitting in exam rooms, I slept sixteen hours a day. There were times when I was so physically and emotionally spent that I wondered if I had any fight left in me at all.

Overwhelm can be paralyzing. When you have too many drains on your physical, emotional, and mental energy, it can feel impossible to gain a single inch, much less make the progress you urgently need.

In those early days, I realized that the only way I could keep going was by breaking the overwhelming days and weeks into smaller chunks. In other words, I learned how to compartmentalize. You can't climb a staircase all at once, but you can do it step by step. This is the magic of compartmentalizing—it makes the seemingly impossible possible.

No one taught me how to compartmentalize. It's something I started doing instinctively. I now know that compartmentalization is a tool people use intentionally to manage overwhelm, whether that overwhelm springs from something joyful like planning a wedding or something unexpected like going through a complex illness.

When I was nineteen, I compartmentalized days by breaking them into smaller pieces. The moment my alarm went off at 4:30 a.m., I'd wake up and focus only on task number one: *Get up.* After I got out of bed, I'd think about task number two: About half the time it was *dialysis for my kidney.* My mom and I had to leave the house for dialysis by 5:00 a.m. three times a week. After dialysis, which consisted of four hours of sleepiness and intense queasiness, I'd return home for task number three: *Get through an afternoon of pure exhaustion and nausea.* Once that had been accomplished, I'd think about task four and five and on and on. This is how I got through a day.

I also compartmentalized my weeks. Going to multiple doctors' appointments a day was wearing me out, so we began designating one day for each. Mondays were kidney day: I'd do my kidney labs and my transplant appointments. I'd only let myself think about kidney issues on that day and nothing else. Tuesdays were for leg and prosthetic appointments. Wednesdays, I visited my audiologist to work on my hearing loss. Then there would be a day my mom and I would talk about bills, insurance, decision-making, and other matters. Breaking these tasks up day by day gave me room to breathe and think more clearly.

Compartmentalizing these tasks let me move forward baby step by baby step. My feelings of overwhelm waned, and I began to think, *I can do this.*

And then I did do it. I made it through.

Not only that, but I went on to use what I'd figured out to get through all the overwhelming seasons that followed.

After compartmentalizing on my own for decades, I learned something remarkable: Retired Navy SEAL commander and trainer of special operations teams Rich Diviney says the one trait shared by all Navy SEALs that accounts for their extraordinary performance is that they are master compartmentalizers.

Compartmentalization is central to Navy SEAL success because it makes any task, no matter how impossible it seems, become achievable.

In his book *Masters of Uncertainty*,[4] Diviney explains that difficult tasks always feature an element of uncertainty. Even when you have a pretty good idea of what needs to be done to complete a task or survive an ordeal—for example, running a marathon—there will always be unknowns. You can't always predict which challenges may crop up during the run, like a leg cramp or dehydration. You don't know how much pain you might experience. You don't know what other obstacles you might have to push through. You don't know how much effort you'll need to finish in your goal time. All these unknowns can create a feeling of overwhelm, even if you've trained for months!

Compartmentalization solves this by training you to complete one step at a time instead of panicking about the unknowns.

When all these new health scares blindsided me so soon after my leg surgery, I compartmentalized. I focused on one appointment at a time and thought about only one issue at a time. I scheduled everything in advance and gave myself breathing room in between each appointment to decompress. When curveballs came, I calmly adapted by rescheduling my day or week. This discipline let me keep my head above water even when I felt sure I was going to drown.

Thank goodness I found that calm in the storm, because ultimately everything turned out fine. All the secondary tests on my thyroid and mammogram were normal. If I'd given in to the overwhelm, I'm not sure I would have made it through without a nervous breakdown.

Compartmentalizing isn't just for hard times; it's also helpful in good times when your life is brimming over with activities you enjoy. I'll often give back-to-back speeches where I'm traveling from one event to the next. I once gave thirteen speeches across thirteen cities in sixteen days. During that whirlwind sequence, I spoke for a company in New York one evening, took a three-hour car ride to Boston early the next morning, gave a speech in Boston later that day, then took a red-eye to California for another company's event the next morning: three speeches in three cities in about thirty-six hours.

The only way I can get through this kind of schedule is to compartmentalize. When I'm traveling, I only let myself think about the talk I'm about to give, not the one that comes after that. It's only the moment I step offstage that I start thinking about the next one.

If I'd looked at my schedule and tried to fathom giving thirteen talks in thirteen cities in sixteen days, I would have said, *There's no way I can do that!* But by taking it one step at a time, one flight at a time, and one speech at a time, I managed it easily without getting overwhelmed.

Compartmentalization has become the defining feature of how I manage my life. I carry one task to completion, then start another one and complete that. Day by day, chunk by chunk, everything gets done.

Whether you're fighting to survive or living the life of your dreams, compartmentalization helps you build a bridge between the possible and the seemingly impossible. When you get into the habit of compartmentalizing, you'll feel less stress and overwhelm when you're facing a major challenge or pursuing an ambitious goal. Instead of getting paralyzed by the enormity of what lies ahead, you'll instinctively know how to break it down into manageable pieces.

And when you finally get to the place you've been aiming for, you'll look back and realize that you couldn't have done it any other way.

TOOL: FIND FOCUS BY COMPARTMENTALIZING

When life feels overwhelming, the solution isn't to tackle everything at once—it's to break things into manageable pieces and handle them one by one. Compartmentalization helps you use your mental and physical resources wisely and efficiently instead of squandering them on panic. Here are my favorite ways to beat overwhelm by compartmentalizing:

1. Prioritize tasks.

Think about your priorities. Which task absolutely needs to get done first? Put it on your schedule, and move less important tasks to later dates.

2. Create time blocks.

Block out times on your calendar to focus on specific tasks. For example, I'll set aside one hour just for writing the introduction to a speech and schedule another part of my talk for later in the day.

Be realistic about how much time the task will take. You want it to be doable in the amount of time you allow for it, without giving it so much time that you lose focus.

Find the sweet spot where there's just enough urgency to motivate you without making you panic.

I also assign myself time blocks for worry. Go ahead and write it in your calendar: "Worry." "Freak out." During that scheduled time, let yourself feel what you need to feel, then move on.

3. Give yourself breathing room.

Instead of booking three important doctor's appointments or other intense tasks on a single day, schedule one a day or one a week. This gives you time to recuperate and bring your most present and capable self to every meeting or task. Spacing out your tasks also gives you time to digest new information, which helps you be more strategic and effective in the long run.

4. Focus on one thing at a time.

Focus on the one thing you need to deal with right now. Set the rest aside for later.

If you're stressed, you might feel tempted to ruminate about everything you have to do later. Don't fall into that trap—it's what made you feel so overwhelmed in the first place.

Keep returning your attention to the present moment. The more attention you give to the task at hand, the better you will execute it. Distraction drains willpower, but focus conserves your energy.

5. Learn to let go.

As soon as you have completed a task, let yourself be done with it, whether it's a job interview, a sales presentation, a doctor's appointment, or even cleaning out your closet. You might be tempted to worry about how it went or to replay events in your head. Don't do this! Most of the time, this kind of rumination doesn't yield much in the way of new insight, and meanwhile, it drains energy from all the tasks you still have in front of you.

Instead, turn your full attention to the next task on your list. Learning to let go quickly makes you efficient, and being efficient reduces overwhelm.

6. Practice self-care.

In the midst of overwhelm, it can be tempting to sleep less, stop cooking nutritious food, let exercise slide, or put off seeing or caring for friends and family. But sleep, exercise, nutrition, and connection are real human needs that help you perform at the highest level. If you don't prioritize them, your best-laid plans will begin to come apart. Take care of yourself. You'll think more clearly, act more calmly, and do a better job of completing each task.

—

Compartmentalization teaches that you can trust yourself to handle whatever's on your plate, just not all at once. When life feels like it's coming at you from every angle, don't shut down—*slow* down. Come back to your center and remember that you don't have to climb the whole mountain in one go. You just have to take the next step. Approaching challenges this way dissolves panic and replaces it with calm, clarity, and the certainty that you *can* get through this.

When it rains, it pours, and it's compartmentalizing that helps you conquer the storm.

FIVE

WEAK AND ALONE to *Supported and Strong*

UP UNTIL THIS INJURY, I'd spent years dragging hundreds of pounds of snowboarding equipment through airports by myself. I insisted on lifting my own luggage, opening my own doors, and strutting through the world on my own two feet. My independence was a key part of my identity. I didn't just take pride in it—it felt like who I *was*.

When the injury happened, I couldn't even brush my teeth without help. Daniel had to bring me a bowl of water while I sat on the couch, because getting to the bathroom sink was just too hard. I couldn't cook, clean, or move around. Sometimes I couldn't brush my own hair. Every time I moved, the pain would flare up, so I barely got off the couch. If we left the house, Daniel pushed me in a wheelchair. It felt like all the independence I'd worked so hard to achieve had vanished overnight.

I'd always been good at accepting help from my mom. She's an extraordinary nurturer who genuinely loves helping me, and I've always let her. To this day, she tells me how grateful she is that I've never pushed her away.

But this injury was the first time I *truly* let Daniel in. After being together for twenty-plus years, we'd been plenty vulnerable with each other. But this injury took that vulnerability to new depths. This time, there was no holding back. I let him see the worst of me: frightened, grieving, bawling my eyes out. He saw me bruised, bleeding profusely, and crawling on the floor to get to the bathroom.

Throughout all this, something unexpected happened: The weaker I was, the stronger we became.

When I realized that Daniel was seeing the worst of me and kept on showing up, that's when I knew deep in my bones that I wasn't alone on this journey.

Hard times can leave you feeling isolated, even if you're surrounded by friends. It can be tempting to shut people out, especially if you're afraid of overwhelming them with your problems. It's all too easy to tell yourself you'll deal with things on your own; after all, you can always let people in *later*, once everything is tidily resolved. But if you really want to strengthen your bonds with others, you need to let people in *during* the difficulty, even (and especially) if it makes you feel exposed.

My vulnerability made it possible for Daniel to show up and meet my needs. He rose to the occasion in a way I'd never seen him do before. It was almost like he'd been waiting for his time to shine. After all these years of asserting my independence and doing so much for myself, I realized I'd never really let Daniel take care of me. This was a little ironic, because there had been times in the past when I'd gotten upset that he wasn't doing more for me. Now I realized it was because I'd never really let him.

In the past, I felt like I was doing the bulk of the cleaning. I'd get annoyed because he didn't do the dishes or other chores often enough. But now Daniel started cleaning more than ever before. He'd get up early every morning to vacuum, dust, wipe surfaces, and tidy up so that I had a clean house to wake up to. I never asked him to do this. He did it because he knew I appreciated it—and my heartfelt appreciation made him want to do it even more!

Daniel also became an excellent chef. We'd always loved cooking together, but now he dove in and leveled up his cooking skills. From the couch, I would watch him in the kitchen with a towel thrown over his shoulder like a professional chef, listening to music, chopping vegetables, flipping food in a pan, and cooking new recipes he found on the internet.

He would present me with a meal that looked like it came from a Michelin-starred restaurant: cilantro lovingly shaped into a flower on top of salsa, tomatoes arranged like a heart on top of a bean and cheese burrito. He often presented these homemade meals to me on a tray with a glass of wine and sometimes even a little flower in a vase.

"Here you go, sweets," he would say with a flourish. "Dinner is served."

I realized Daniel *loved* taking care of me. I saw a whole new nurturing side of him I hadn't yet experienced—one I don't think even *he* had known was there. His enjoyment made him thrive as a caregiver, and this sparked a new realization in me: I loved being taken care of too.

I now realize that at the peak of my independence, Daniel hadn't felt like I needed him, because I'd created the perception for both me and him that I didn't. The reality, however, is that we needed and still need each other.

This experience brought our intimacy and love for each other to a new depth. In fact, when many couples were separating during the COVID-19 pandemic, Daniel and I were closer than we had ever been, glued to each other's side, functioning almost symbiotically. I needed his help, he helped me, I appreciated him, and he felt appreciated. Who would have thought that times of weakness can actually make you so strong?

During this time, I also got vulnerable with my friend Jack Hollis, the North American vice president of my sponsor, Toyota. One day while we were texting about my injury, I asked if he could talk. We got on a call, and I told him how scared I was about the outcome of an upcoming surgery. He asked if he could pray for me, and I welcomed it. We prayed together. We cried together. And then he and Toyota not only vowed to continue to be my partner but also became family for life.

All of this made me feel supported and gave me strength when I needed it most. At first, being so open about what I was going through made me feel exposed. But when I noticed how deeply my vulnerability allowed me to connect with Daniel and with people like Jack, I began thinking about how I could be more vulnerable with my online community as well. If I let them in more, could we all benefit from it?

Being truly vulnerable on social media takes tremendous courage, whether you have five followers or five million. When we go through hard times, it's tempting to withdraw until the storm passes, then emerge to share a triumphant survival story with a pretty red bow around it. It feels way safer to say, "I went through something tough, but now I'm better," than to say, "I'm in the thick of it right now and have no idea where this is going."

But when we open our inner world for others to see, we make space for them to step in and support us, and we give ourselves the opportunity to connect with people who've had similar experiences.

I started sharing my journey on Instagram in real time. Each morning, I'd wake up and post what was on my mind. One day I'd share how anxiety had kept me up all night, along with small things that helped me cope. Another day, I'd share a specific fear and explain how I was dealing with it. Sometimes I even shared moments of total vulnerability, like an image of my shoulders in the bath with my head down, with a caption that explained how afraid I was of not knowing if I would walk again.

I felt so exposed sharing that photo, and yet the amount of support that poured in was unbelievable. People responded to my posts saying things like, "Oh my gosh, thank you for sharing, Amy! I have anxiety too, and this is how I handle it!" Or, "Thank you for sharing, Amy! I thought I was the only one who felt this way. Thank you for helping me feel seen and not so alone."

I poured my heart out, and people poured their hearts into me. I was always careful to make sure my purpose on social media was to inspire people and give them hope, not just unload my pain. But when people responded by sharing their own struggles and flooding me with their support, we became a community. I needed that strength and support more than they could imagine.

I remembered the first time I'd glimpsed the power of vulnerability, when I gave a TEDx Talk in 2011.[5]

It was my first big talk, and I was terrified to go on such a grand stage and share my story with the world. I was especially scared to share the hard parts. Back then, I couldn't even say the words "I lost my legs" without tearing up. When I was preparing my talk, my first instinct was to breeze through the parts that made me emotional. But after working with a speaking coach who encouraged me to go deeper, I wrote the talk with my whole heart. Right before stepping onstage, she whispered, "Amy, remember, if you feel it, the audience will too."

When I stepped into the spotlight, I released my fear, opened my heart, and poured myself out completely. I kept speaking even when my voice cracked and my eyes filled with tears. I let the audience witness my real emotions as I felt them. Through my tears, I looked into the audience and saw that the first three rows of people had tears in their eyes too. An older man had even lifted his glasses to wipe his face.

This speech ended up going viral and changing the course of my life forever. It launched me into a corporate speaking career that continues to grow to this day.

My TED Talk was a moment when vulnerability didn't just save me from a low but powered me to higher highs—in fact, my *highest* of highs. It started me on a journey of making the most impact I can with my story and the lessons I've learned. Being willing to go into the world and be vulnerable taught me just how important it is to share our stories, our fears, and our insecurities, even the ones we're scared to talk about, because those are what make us human, and what makes us human connects us all.

Brené Brown defines vulnerability as uncertainty, risk, and emotional exposure. It's showing your soft underbelly and opening yourself to being wounded. But vulnerability is also, in her words, "the birthplace of love, belonging, joy, courage, empathy, and creativity."[6] She's right.

I will add to that list resilience. Vulnerability is not the only place from which resilience springs. But it is a powerful reservoir of it, because it enables us to feel bonded and safe, to build trust, and to know we aren't alone—we have others to fight for while they fight for us.

Vulnerability isn't easy for me. It's not easy for most of us. It means taking off the mask you've been hiding behind, breaking down the walls that separate you from others, and showing your true self even if it's not your best self.

But here's what I've learned: All humans are stronger together, and embracing that truth lets us form deeper bonds. The more we open up about our needs, the more we build relationships that can actually help us meet them.

The neuroscience is clear: Our minds and bodies are wired for connection. Take oxytocin, the hormone associated with feelings of love and safety. Our bodies produce oxytocin when we have experiences that deepen trust with others, and this has been linked to lower blood pressure,[7] improved sleep,[8] and a stronger immune system. Oxytocin also helps regulate the stress response and appears to lower stress hormone levels,[9] contributing to a calmer, more relaxed state.

We become more physically and emotionally resilient when we're willing to be vulnerable and connect at the deepest level. I find it fascinating that the very thing that makes us feel unsafe at first—vulnerability—is the same thing that creates true safety.

Vulnerability allows you to receive instead of resist. It helps transform your weakest times into your strongest moments. It creates resilience by forging stronger relationships and reminding us that we aren't on this journey alone.

Release your resistance and you will receive resilience. Simply put: Let love in.

TOOL: EMBRACE VULNERABILITY

Deciding to be vulnerable means letting go of your pride—and being willing to trust that others won't hurt you. Vulnerability builds the kind of deep, authentic relationships that can carry you through any challenge and reveal just how loved and supported you really are. Here are a few tips to get you started practicing vulnerability:

1. Develop self-awareness.

You can't be vulnerable about your emotions with others if you're not even sure what you're feeling. Start by developing self-awareness. Practice getting curious about your emotions and naming what you feel. Are you feeling hurt? Angry? Embarrassed? Once you've put your finger on the emotion, stay with it and *feel* it.

Fully feeling your emotions can be uncomfortable, but that's okay. Discomfort doesn't typically harm you; it can actually make you grow. When you understand what you're feeling and release self-judgment for it, it's easier to let other people in.

2. Own your imperfections.

None of us are perfect, and nothing is more human than going through adversity. Let yourself be imperfect. In fact, celebrate your flaws—they're part of what makes you *you*.

Accepting your imperfections lets you reclaim all the energy you spent trying to hide them from other people. Deep self-acceptance makes it easier to open up to others, because even if *they* don't accept you (which is unlikely) at least you know that *you* accept you.

The more you share your honest and vulnerable self, the more other people feel comfortable sharing their honest and vulnerable selves with you. Far from being put off by your vulnerability, they think, *Thank God I can take off this uncomfortable mask and show up as my true self too.*

3. Practice courage.

It takes courage to put yourself out there exactly as you are. The only way to build this kind of courage is to practice it.

Practice opening up to others. It's okay to start small. Choose people with whom you think it could be safe to share your thoughts and emotions, like close friends, family, or other members of your inner circle. You can start sharing things gradually and open up more over time.

You could also try vulnerability with strangers if that feels safer, since you may never cross paths with them again. For example, in the past I never let people help me lift things into my car. But now that I use a little scooter to get around since my injury, strangers often ask me if I need help. Instead of snapping back, "No, I've got it!," I let them help. Doing this has relieved some of the pressure I feel and has also helped me remember how many kind people there are in the world.

4. Ask for help.

Practice asking for help. You'll be surprised how many people light up when you finally give them the chance to show how much they care about you.

People love to help—they really do. One of my friends likes to say, "Gift people the gift of gifting you." It is only through our willingness to receive that other people can experience the joys of giving. Helping others makes us feel happy and gives us purpose, so why deprive your friends and family of those gifts?

We weren't meant to be islands going through life alone. Vulnerability is a dance of mutual caring. Sometimes one person does more giving than another in one season, but then a new season comes and the balance shifts back. This constant exchange is what makes us human.

5. Be honest.

Being honest with yourself and others is the key to vulnerability. You can't be genuinely vulnerable if you're only telling half the truth or hiding behind a false persona.

When you show up as your authentic self, you build trust with the people around you, welcoming them into a place of deep connection.

Remember: What makes you feel vulnerable makes you human, and what makes us human connects us all.

—

The more you practice self-acceptance, vulnerability becomes less about feeling frighteningly exposed and more about welcoming authentic connection with other people. Although it may feel safer to hide your struggles until they're neatly resolved, letting others be with you through the messy parts will strengthen your relationships, deepen your trust, and dissolve the illusion that you're alone. The moment you realize that people don't abandon you when you show your weak parts but actually draw closer, you'll realize you never have to carry your burdens alone.

SIX

FEARING THE UNKNOWN to *Believing in the Possibilities*

I LIVED ON THE COUCH for four months before even *thinking* about trying to wear a prosthetic on my injured leg again. When the time finally came, Daniel and I trekked to my prosthetic shop in Denver, where Zach Harvey, my prosthetist at the time, had me test out a new leg system. I was excited but felt some trepidation. I knew my leg still wasn't back to normal. Just that morning I'd caught a glimpse of it in the mirror and saw that it was purple. But I took a deep breath and squared my shoulders. There was no way to know for sure how the appointment would go until I got there. So I went.

First, we rolled on the liner (which is snug). This was supposed to be the easy part. Once the liner was on, we sat there and waited for a few minutes. Then we took it off again to see how my leg had responded. The bottom of my leg had turned completely white—a sign there wasn't enough blood flow. My heart sank.

From all my years of experience, I knew if I couldn't wear a liner, there was no way I could wear a prosthetic.

My stomach twisted into knots. *I may never walk again on my own two feet*, I thought.

Zach immediately recommended I see a friend of his, Dr. Omar Mubarak. Dr. Mubarak was not just a vascular surgeon but also an athlete who'd completed two Ironman triathlons. Zach thought he might be able to pick up where Dr. Cooper had left off and help make my leg healthier so that I could one day walk in my prosthetic again.

Dr. Mubarak rearranged his schedule to see me as soon as possible. The moment he walked through the door, brimming with positive energy, it was clear he was everything Zach had made him out to be. After quick introductions, he leaped right into explaining his ideas about what we could do.

"I've reviewed Dr. Cooper's notes," he said. "Even though your vessels are clear, they've shrunk to such a small size that barely any blood can get through."

I braced myself for him to tell me there was nothing he could do. But then he said, "I think we can increase blood flow by going in there and creating more room in the vessels. We can blast through them if we have to!"

I immediately thought, *This is my guy!* I told him I was in.

The next day, I went to the hospital for an angiogram. This would help Dr. Mubarak determine why my leg got a blood clot in the first place—a question nobody had been able to answer. He found significant damage and scar tissue behind my knee and to my popliteal artery, which runs through the knee to the lower leg. This suggested my popliteal artery had closed due to injury.

When Dr. Mubarak told me this, I flashed back to a day about a month before the injury when I had experienced an unusual and intense pain in my upper calf while snowboarding. I also remembered that when walking in my heels at the Golden Globes, my upper calf hurt in an unusual way. In fact, I'd spent the evening sitting down every chance I could.

Dr. Mubarak explained that these incidents hadn't caused the damage to my artery. Rather, they were the first major signs that it had already happened. In fact, this problem had most likely been brewing for many years—I just hadn't realized it.

It turns out my prosthetic had always been slightly too tight in the upper calf, behind my knee. As Dr. Mubarak and I discussed this, I remembered how throughout all my years of snowboarding, hiking, and walking through airports, I'd always felt pressure behind that knee. My calf had felt sore sometimes, too, but I had thought it was only from bruising my calf muscle from the pressure of my prosthetic, not actually injuring my popliteal artery. (And yes, if you are confused about my calves, as a below-the-knee amputee I still have about eleven inches of my leg below the knee, including my shin and calf.)

I never suspected that this minor, constant pressure would end up severely injuring me. Had I known that an injury of this magnitude was possible, I would have had my prosthetic adjusted to relieve the pressure. But there was no way to go back in time to reverse what had been done—and no time for regrets.

Okay. Now we know. Time to move forward, I thought.

After the angiogram, I went straight into a medical-grade hyperbaric oxygen chamber, part of Dr. Mubarak's plan to coax my body into growing new blood vessels.

I returned to this chamber three hours a day, five days a week for the next three months. Daniel and I even rented an apartment in Denver to make the trip easier. We were all in.

After several months of working with Dr. Mubarak, my leg showed some signs of improvement. But the lack of blood flow at the very bottom created atrophy. I lost muscle, fat, and cushion in the area. My tibia bone was nearly sticking through my skin. I thought, *There's no way I'll be able to walk in a prosthetic like this.*

Dr. Mubarak agreed that I'd need to have what's known in the surgical world as a revision to shorten my leg before I'd have any hope of fitting a prosthetic. I wouldn't need the full-on above-the-knee amputation I was so scared of. But some amount of my leg would have to be shortened to capture as much blood flow as possible. The vessels at the bottom were just too small and damaged. Exactly how much had to come off would depend on the opinion and skill of whomever I found to do the surgery. This scared me, but there was no other way.

I began reaching out to surgeons. I also contacted my friend Hugh Herr, who is a double-leg amputee himself and also the cohead of the K. Lisa Yang Center for Bionics at the Massachusetts Institute of Technology. Hugh put me in touch with a surgeon named Dr. Matthew Carty, with whom he was developing a new experimental amputation. Dr. Carty is a world-renowned reconstructive plastic surgeon who had worked with many of the survivors who'd lost limbs in the Boston Marathon bombing. Dr. Carty and I soon got on a video call to discuss my options.

Instead of the typical amputation where you cut the muscles and bone, which leaves the muscles unable to work again and makes them more likely to atrophy, the technique Hugh and Dr. Carty had been developing involved connecting the protagonist and antagonist muscles to each other so that the muscles could continue to work. The muscles could flex and build themselves, and this, Dr. Carty explained, would in theory encourage blood to flow down to the furthest parts of my leg.

That was exactly what I needed.

Daniel and I immediately made plans to head to Boston for the month of August so that I could undergo surgery.

Knowing I had done everything I could to preserve the full length of my leg, I resolved to completely embrace this amputation. And yet

I still felt a mix of negative emotions heading into it. One was grief. I felt deeply sad about losing more of the leg that had taken me so far in life. I drew many baths to submerge myself in the hot water and mourn the loss. These legs had taken me to some amazing places. I had worked so hard to win freedom and abilities few had considered attainable. I realized that I felt just as attached to my prosthetic legs as I was to the legs I'd been born with.

I also felt a renewed fear of the unknown. I knew this amputation needed to be done, but the surgery was experimental, and we couldn't be sure it would work or that it would fully fix the blood flow issue. Even if it did work, it's incredibly difficult to get prosthetics to fit well enough to be able to do all the activities I loved. I worried that the process would take years and that my new prosthetic would never fit as well as the old one, therefore limiting my abilities. I wondered, *Will I ever snowboard as well as I did before? Will walking ever feel so natural again?*

It just so happened that my revision surgery took place on the twentieth anniversary of losing my legs in the first place. Who would have ever thought that exactly twenty years later I would be here again? Life is wild.

When Dr. Carty's surgical team shortened and fully reconstructed the muscles of my lower leg, I was under the knife for eight hours. When I woke up, my leg was now enclosed in a brace I would wear for the next eight weeks, and I was in significant pain. Emotionally, I felt lost at sea. This was a level of uncertainty beyond anything I'd faced before. I had lost my footing—both literally and figuratively.

The apartment Daniel and I had rented in Boston was beautiful, especially the floor-to-ceiling glass windows, which showcased the most amazing sunrises and sunsets I'd ever seen. As I recovered over the next eight weeks with my mom and Daniel by my side, I would stare out the window for hours and let my mind wander. I imagined I had stepped onto a boat and floated out to sea, with no idea where this ship was going to sail. I felt as if I were floating out toward the horizon, with no plan, no direction, just seeing where the tide would take me.

The one thing I knew for sure was that I was starting over from scratch, which made me nervous. Just because I had done amazing things on my prosthetic legs before was no guarantee that I could do it again.

I found some comfort in a quote I once heard: "The unknown is where possibilities live."

I had already done the best I could with the situation I was in. It was time for me to step into the sea of possibilities. Who knew what would come next? It was more important than ever for me to believe that I would be okay no matter where I ended up.

A lot of people think that believing in yourself means believing in specific skills or talents, like your ability to snowboard or give a speech. To me, believing in myself means trusting I can get through whatever comes my way. And the foundation of that belief is knowing that no matter what happens, even if things go badly or I make "mistakes," I will learn and grow. I will stay agile and handle whatever comes: wave after wave, storm after storm, uncertain sea after uncertain sea.

While sitting in that beautiful apartment gazing out at the cityscape and sky, I realized that believing in my ability to learn and grow had been the key to my successes. In many of my proudest moments, such as relearning how to snowboard, competing on *Dancing with the Stars*, winning medals, and beginning a public speaking career, I remembered that I was able to do all those things because I believed in my heart that I *could*, even if I didn't always know *how* I'd do it.

I'd figure it out! I'd *learn*. I'd grow.

This time was no different.

I now know that this attitude is called a growth mindset. A growth mindset is the belief that you can learn, grow, and change for the better. Carol Dweck, the pioneering psychologist who coined the term, put it beautifully in her book *Mindset: The New Psychology of Success*: "The passion for stretching yourself and sticking to it, even (or especially) when it's not going well, is the hallmark of the growth mindset. This is the mindset that allows people to thrive during some of the most challenging times in their lives."[10]

The opposite of a growth mindset, a fixed mindset, is believing that you are who you are and that will never change.

Have you ever said or heard someone say, "I'm not a math person" or "I could never get up in front of people and speak; I'm horrible at that"?

This is a fixed mindset: the belief that you are fixed in a certain way and that it's not going to change.

A growth mindset sounds more like this: "I may not like math, but I'm sure if I worked hard enough, I could figure it out."

Or this: "I am terrified to get up in front of people and speak, but that doesn't mean I can't do it."

A growth mindset means believing that it's not natural-born talent that gets you somewhere—it's hard work. You may not yet know how to accomplish the task in front of you, but you know that if you keep working at it, you'll figure it out.

Many people have confidence in specific skills: *I'm good at sports* or *I know I can win over even the most difficult customers.* This type of self-assurance is great, but an even more powerful form of confidence is confidence in your ability to learn and grow from whatever challenges come your way: *I can confront any new challenge and figure it out.* This type of self-confidence helps you in *all* circumstances, whether or not you're doing something you're "good" at.

A growth mindset makes all the difference in the world when you're facing down an uncertain future. If you believe in your ability to rise to the occasion and learn whatever skills you need to meet new challenges, you're all but guaranteed to succeed.

Believe that you will figure things out, even if you don't yet know how. Trust that you'll be able to get through uncertain times—*and you will.* It's like one of my favorite quotes (attributed to Henry Ford): "Whether you believe you can, or you believe you can't, you're right." Humans rise to the occasion. We do what we must. Twenty years ago, I figured things out. I knew, with this latest surgery, that I could do it again.

Choosing a growth mindset not only builds resilience so that you can keep moving forward but also paves the way for you to become a new and improved version of yourself.

TOOL: HARNESS THE POWER OF BELIEF

If you ever find yourself facing the unknown, remember that opportunities you didn't even know existed are waiting for you to find them. What feels like a scary void is actually an invitation to create something new. When you believe in your own ability to rise to any occasion, life becomes way less daunting. Here are three tips to help you harness the power of belief and step more boldly into the unknown:

1. Adopt a growth mindset.

Next time something doesn't go as planned and you're frustrated or feel like giving up, ask yourself, *What can I learn from this? Is there a skill I can work on that will make me more likely to succeed if I try again?*

When you start asking yourself, *How can I learn, and how can I grow from this?*, you can step into the unknown with greater confidence.

There's really no chance you will "fail" because no matter what happens, you will learn something that helps you do better next time, and that's an outcome worth celebrating.

When you begin *believing* that you can do more and are made for more, even if you don't know what that "more" is, the path will start to reveal itself.

2. Be mindful.

Mindfulness means paying attention to what you're thinking and how your brain works. When you're being mindful, you can catch yourself when you slip into a fixed mindset and choose a growth mindset instead.

Make a habit of watching your thoughts. You can practice this while meditating, doing yoga, or sitting in silence like I did when I was gazing out the window in Boston. If you catch yourself in a negative thought pattern, ask yourself, *Is what I'm thinking getting me closer to my goals or farther away from them?* or *Am I believing in the possibilities right now, or am I limiting what's possible?*

Whenever you hear yourself say you can't do something or find yourself rejecting an idea about what's possible, stop yourself and finish the sentence in a way that helps you focus on the possibilities ahead.

3. Add *yet* to the end of your negative thought.

When you catch yourself thinking or saying something limiting, add the word *yet*. Then follow up the limiting thought with a possibility. For example:

"I'm in pain and can't walk . . . yet! Day by day I'm getting better."

"I'm not cut out for this job . . . yet! Eventually I will figure it out."

"I can't stand in front of people and speak . . . at least not yet! Eventually, with hard work, I will do it."

"I can't do algebra . . . yet! If I get a tutor, I'm sure I will master it."

The magical *yet* gives you room to grow.

I love the word *yet* because it reminds me that I'm never stuck in my present condition—I can learn and grow and try new things in new ways. So many possibilities reveal themselves to us when we embrace our own ability to change and grow.

—

The power of belief is knowing that *you can do this,* whatever the *this* may be. You may feel lost at sea today, but you will find your way to shore. And you never know: That new shore may be more beautiful than the one you left behind and teeming with possibilities you never could have imagined.

SEVEN

CRITICIZING YOUR BODY to *Celebrating It*

OVER THE NEXT THREE YEARS, I went through numerous surgeries in the fight to save my leg. Dr. Mubarak would go into the artery, stretch it out, open things up, and allow more blood to pass through. Eventually, the artery would close, we'd open it back up, and it would stay clear for a few months. Then it would randomly block up again. I knew in the back of my mind that there may eventually be nothing we could do to stop this from happening, but for the time being, I wasn't ready to surrender. I was still committed to the fight.

For many of these procedures, I was awake—feeling everything and talking to Dr. Mubarak (who became a great friend) as he made an incision in my right groin and entered my femoral artery. He would use a wirelike tool that would move up through the artery in my abdomen all the way over to my left leg and down below the knee.

Because we were dealing with arteries, there was a lot of blood thinner involved. This meant a lot of bleeding. To stop the bleeding, Dr. Mubarak's team would hold my femoral artery down painfully hard for ten minutes after closing up the area. But sometimes the bleeding would continue under my skin and down into my muscle, causing a giant hematoma (a deep muscle bruise). It hurt, and it *looked* like it hurt.

One time after returning home from one of these procedures, I lay in bed for several days before even standing up on my crutches because I had so much pain in the incision area. When I finally did get up, the first thing I did was crutch to the bathroom and look in the mirror.

I was met with a reflection of a person I didn't recognize: a pale, rail-thin girl who looked like she'd been to hell and back. I was skin and bones. I could count my ribs. I felt like I had fought for my life, and I looked like it too.

I had a massive black-and-blue bruise that started at my belly button and stretched all the way down my inner right thigh to my knee. It was from an unusually severe hematoma that had developed in my right artery after the latest procedure—and that was on my "good" leg.

As for my injured leg, there was a three-inch-long purple scar that ran across my left upper thigh. It stood out bright against my pale skin, still fresh from initial surgery back in February.

As I stared at my reflection, my spirit wilted. In my mind, I was still an athlete: strong and fit. Fully capable. Whole. Yet seeing the evidence of all I had endured, I felt sad for myself and all my body had gone through.

I said out loud, "Oh my God, you are so weak and broken, Amy."

Sadness flooded me. With tears in my eyes, I crutched over to the toilet, collapsed onto it, and dropped my head into my hands.

I sat in sorrow, trying to wrap my head around the vision of what my body had become. But after only twenty seconds, I had this thought: *Amy, do the opposite of what you are doing right now.*

The thought felt powerful and authoritative, so I immediately said back to myself, *Okay*, and replaced the thoughts I was having with their opposites.

Instead of saying, "I am weak," I said, "I am strong."

Instead of saying, "My body is broken," I said, "No, Amy, your body is unbelievably resilient! Look at all it has endured!"

Instantly, my mood began to lift. The change was remarkable. The more I praised my body, the more my appreciation for it grew.

I started thinking about just how resilient and incredible my body was. It had gotten me through the time when I lost my legs, kidneys, and spleen all at once, and it had bounced back to become stronger than it ever was before. The more I thought about how much my body had done for me over the years, the more a sense of awe began to blossom inside me.

I began to marvel at the ways my body was constantly fighting for me. Take that three-inch scar on my thigh, for example. I wasn't exactly happy about how gnarly it looked, but I thought, *Wow, just think of all the processes in my body that pulled together to make that scar form. My body was wounded, and it mended itself!*

And what about that huge bruise down my inner thigh? Although it looked and felt nasty, it was healing itself by spreading and breaking up. Bruises are part of the healing process, and my body was doing exactly what it was made to do: heal.

I said to myself, "Thank you, body, for fighting so hard for me."

Our brains are always listening to us, and they believe what we tell them. They'll even believe the opinions we give them over the facts. Consider this: *I have a scar* is a fact. *My scar is ugly* is an opinion. *My body is ugly* is also an opinion, not a fact. The fact is simply: *I have a body.*

When we tell our brains opinions like these, they put them on equal footing with objective facts. Then, because our brains are wired to seek evidence for facts, they start looking for supporting data. This means that a stranger might look at a scar on your leg and have wonder or appreciation on their face, but if you've already given your brain the opinion *my scar is ugly*, you'll construe that look as judgment or disgust because you've primed your brain to interpret it that way.

The good news is that we have the power to choose how we talk to ourselves. We can influence our brains to believe things that serve us or things that break us down. So why not be your biggest cheerleader instead of your biggest critic?

Most of the things we say to ourselves about our bodies are opinions. However, there is one fact about all our bodies that overrides all possible opinions we might have about them: Our bodies are amazingly resilient.

They are survivors. Warriors. Allies that give us the gift of life.

They are always fighting for us.

They are miracles.

It's important to remind ourselves of this fact, especially in a time when we're bombarded with media images of idealized (and often airbrushed) bodies that are designed to make us feel broken, ugly, or desperately in need of fixing.

Our bodies are fighting for us every single moment of our lives. They are our greatest allies, but most of the time, we are such jerks to them. Our bodies show up for us each day, fixing wounds, repairing damage, giving us fat as an energy reserve or as a cushion to stay warm, and yet we rarely appreciate their hard work. Instead, we talk down to them.

But they are *brilliant*! Our bodies contain trillions of cells working in perfect harmony across the immune, digestive, respiratory, cardiovascular, nervous, sensory, skeletal, and muscular systems. As they weather the damage of going through daily life, they're in constant repair mode, providing us with the amazing gift of being alive. This symphony of healing is always happening, yet most of the time we don't notice or appreciate it.

Our bodies are miracles in action, and every "flaw" we see is a beautiful reminder of their ability to heal us.

On top of experiencing meningitis, septic shock, kidney failure, amputation, and hearing loss when I was nineteen, I've faced other challenges as an athlete. In 2016, I endured rhabdomyolysis, an injury caused by overexerting muscles. This took several months of rest and recovery to heal from. I also experienced a nerve inflammatory disorder in both arms called brachial neuritis in 2017, which resulted in major muscle loss that took ten months of physical therapy and major changes in my nutrition to heal.

Rather than viewing these moments as evidence of brokenness, I see them as evidence of amazing strength. My darkest moments physically are the moments when my body has shown me just how extraordinary it is.

No matter what your body is going through—an injury, a metabolic condition, an infection, or stress—it's doing everything it can to keep you alive. It may not always seem like it, but that's because healing is not a straight line—believe me, I know firsthand. It's like the stock market: There are small wins, big crashes, huge gains, detours, and setbacks, all while slowly inching forward. Healing is never linear and always comprises two steps forward and one step back. This is the dance of healing, and this dance continues throughout our entire lives.

Sometimes our bodies do break. Sometimes it feels like they betray us. Sometimes they do the opposite of what we want them to do. Sometimes they put us in pain. Regardless, it's all part of their drive to survive. That is always their goal: repair, refresh, strengthen, and move forward. They do this automatically, all day, every day, whether or not we thank them for it. What better ally could we ask for?

Another big thing I've realized? Bodies don't care what they look like! Your body doesn't know that that giant bruise isn't the perfect match for your new dress; it's focused on keeping you alive, warm, and safe, and it's doing a darn good job.

The more we take care of our bodies through proper health, sleep, and nutrition, the more they will take care of us. It's not about being at war with your amazing body. It's about being its *teammate.*

Your body is doing its part. Are you doing yours?

TOOL: CELEBRATE YOUR BODY'S RESILIENCE

Your body is perfectly designed and miraculously resilient. Every single day, it's working to keep you alive—adapting, healing, and carrying you forward. Whether you're sleeping, walking, or just breathing, millions of invisible processes are happening to support your existence here on Earth. Here are two ways to celebrate your body and all that it does for you:

1. Practice the mirror exercise.

This exercise helps you transform negative self-talk by consciously rewiring how you see your body.

1. Stand in front of the mirror where you can see your entire body. Don't cover up the parts you don't like. The idea is to see everything, *especially* the parts that bother you.

2. Look at the parts of your body that make you feel insecure, and pay attention to the first thought that pops into your head.

3. If the thought is negative—for example, *My body is broken*, *My thighs look fat*, *I look and feel weak*, or *That scar is so ugly*—ask yourself, *How can I flip this into a positive thought that celebrates my body's strength instead of tearing it down?*

4. Swap out the negative thought for a positive thought.

Turn *My thighs look fat* to *My body is doing what it was made to do. It's protecting me, keeping me warm, and helping me survive.*

Turn *I look weak* to *My body is so strong. Look at all it does for me every single day. My body will build more muscle when it has the capacity to do so.*

Turn *My chronic health condition means my body is broken* to *My body is persevering in difficult conditions. It's doing the best it can, fighting to keep me alive the best it knows how.*

If you have scars, consider the intricate systems that work together to form a scar: from one group of cells creating a scab to stop you from bleeding, to another group of cells creating a matrix of scaffolding to begin building collagen and elastin, to another group of cells performing angiogenesis, which allows new vessels to grow into the injured area.

You can try this thought: *My cells are like little workers, and I have trillions of them working on me at all times, keeping me going.*

If that doesn't make you appreciate your body, I don't know what will!

5. After all of this, tell your body, *Thank you for all that you are doing for me. I wouldn't be here without you. I vow to take care of you tenderly, as you take care of me.*

Every time you do this exercise, you're rewiring your brain to think differently. Choose new thoughts, and your brain will begin to embrace them.

2. Write a Dear Body letter.

As I was recovering from one of my multiple surgeries, I was asked to model for a swimsuit company. At first, I wasn't sure if I was ready. With all the medical drama going on, I certainly didn't feel *swimsuit-ready.* I felt like my formerly perky athletic butt was now sagging down to my knees, and that was just the start of my insecure thoughts and feelings.

However, I like taking opportunities to step out of my comfort zone, so I chose to do it.

Days before the shoot, they asked me to write a letter to my body that would start with the line "Dear Body . . ."

This ended up being one of the most therapeutic things I've ever done for myself. In fact, while we were doing the shoot, I could barely read it out loud because it made me so emotional.

Here is my Dear Body letter:

> Dear Body,
>
> What an incredible adventure we have been on together.
>
> You've strengthened me when I needed support. You weakened when it was time to rest. You've adapted when it was time to change. You have always found a way to not just survive but thrive. And you have never, not once, given up on me.
>
> Every scar, every stretch mark has saved my life. They are constant reminders of just how resilient you are. It's funny how the world celebrates bodies without imperfections. Yet it's those nicks and marks that represent just how perfect you really are, because those battle wounds are what's left when the battle has been won.
>
> There are times when I try to hide you, to protect you from the world's looks and questions. But now I know that you were never meant to be ordinary because you, my body, are extraordinary. And I love the story that you tell.
>
> My body, you are a miracle.

Try writing a letter like this for yourself. Express your appreciation for your body and all it has done for you. Allow yourself to become vulnerable; in fact, the more vulnerable you get, the more wounds you will heal.

What would *your* Dear Body letter say?

—

Your body is your most loyal teammate, and your brain is always listening to what you say about it. So be your greatest ally—show up and do your part. The words you speak to yourself in the mirror, the opinions you express, and the choices you make about rest and nourishment are all messages you're sending to your body about its worth. Your body is always fighting for you, and the more you take care of it with kindness, the more it will take care of you.

EIGHT

SELF-CRITICISM to *Self-Love*

WHAT THE HELL IS WRONG WITH YOU, Amy? You're usually so motivated, so why aren't you now? There's so much you could and should be doing. Come on, pull it together!

Believe it or not, the person saying these horrible things to me was myself.

It was a Friday morning a few months after the major reconstructive amputation I'd undergone in Boston. I'd been wanting to work on some projects since Monday but hadn't done any of them; I just couldn't bring myself to do them. I had zero motivation, even though I had a huge to-do list.

I kept telling myself, *Amy, you aren't doing enough. You should be doing more.*

I had thoughts like *You should be tackling all your chores and projects. You should be working out. You should be writing another book.*

Yet at the moment, I couldn't even get out of my pajamas or brush my hair.

I'd tried to get going but hadn't made it very far. On Wednesday, I'd forced myself to get up and put on makeup, but then I'd put my pajamas back on and gone back to sleep.

For the rest of the week, questions like *What's wrong with me?* and

Why do I feel this way? played like a broken record in my mind.

I don't usually recommend asking yourself the question *What's wrong with me?*, but in this moment it just so happened to lead somewhere productive. I took a deep breath and tried to find an honest answer to explain why I felt so sluggish.

Why *wasn't* I feeling motivated? Why *couldn't* I do the work?

What were the reasons I was feeling so low?

By asking myself good questions, I got good answers:

My leg was still in pain.

I felt discouraged, and it seemed like every time I began to think my leg was healing, it would suddenly get cold, numb, or painful again.

I was tired of undergoing surgeries and making life-altering decisions.

And to top it all off, my dear friend Bibian had recently received the prognosis that her cancer had spread and that she had only a few weeks left to live.

As I lay in bed staring at the ceiling, I realized that the reason I wasn't motivated was because I was depleted. My body was taking energy to heal. My mind was taking energy to function. My emotions were taking energy to respond to all I was going through, especially the fact that I would soon be losing a dear friend.

Wow, I thought. *I am being incredibly judgmental and cruel to myself.*

The answer to the question *What's wrong with me?* was *Nothing!*

The answer to the question *What should I be doing right now?* was *Nothing!*

I realized that I would never talk to a friend or loved one the way I'd been talking to myself. I would never say, "What's wrong with you? You should be doing so much more with your life!" I would point out everything that person was going through and encourage them to simply relax and heal. A book can wait until later, for heaven's sake.

This moment of self-awareness inspired me to take myself down a different path.

I got up, made myself a latte, and got in the bath.

Then, as if I were talking to a friend, I said to myself, *Amy, you are doing amazingly well considering all you have been through this year. Most importantly, you are doing the best you can.*

You've continued to move forward even with these surgeries and setbacks. Now is not the season of epic accomplishments. Now is the season to hunker down and weather the storm. It's the season to take care of yourself. You are exactly where you need to be. And if there ever was a time to give yourself a little grace, it's right now.

Amy, if there is anything you should be doing right now, it's this.

I'm generally pretty kind to myself, but because I'm a perfectionist and an overachiever, I can also be strict and demanding. I can push myself harder than is healthy and have unreasonably high expectations for how much I can accomplish. And when I slip into that mode, I can develop a harsher than usual tone.

But in that bathtub in the middle of the afternoon, latte in hand, I explored what it meant to give myself grace.

The Bible says grace is the love and mercy given to us by God. I wondered, *What about the grace we give to ourselves?*

It's so easy to give others grace. When someone we love or care about is upset or hurt, we respond with gentleness and care. So why is it so hard to extend that same compassion to ourselves?

I reached out to my friend Liz Gilbert to ask her advice on grace and self-love.[11] You may know Liz from her famous book *Eat, Pray, Love.* Liz and I met while I was speaking on Oprah's *Life You Want Tour* a few years before. She went on to become a mentor and one of my wisest friends.

Liz shared that she'd struggled with a harsh relationship with herself when she was in her early thirties. She'd felt herself "failing" in ways she'd been taught to fear, and this caused her to fall into a long season of darkness and heavy depression. Liz told me that although she eventually got help through therapy, antidepressants, and spiritual practices, the first and most important thing she did was find mercy for herself.

Sometimes people talk about forgiving themselves for their flaws or mistakes. But Liz prefers the language of mercy, as do I. Forgiveness implies that there was some kind of wrong perpetrated. Mercy is different: It's total understanding, empathy, and compassion, with no judgments about right and wrong.

In Liz's words, mercy takes place when "a full pardon is given, but a pardon isn't even needed. You are doing what everyone is doing: experiencing the dilemma of your humanity. And you don't know what to do, and why should you? Because none of us do."

Another thing Liz and I discussed was the importance of being a friend to ourselves. Self-love can be difficult, especially when you hold yourself to excessively high standards like I often do. Loving yourself can feel like too tall an order—but being a friend to ourselves? That's something we can all do. We can all give ourselves the same grace, empathy, kindness, and compassion we would give any of our friends or family.

Be your own best friend and biggest cheerleader. The harsh and judgmental tone your inner critic uses to keep you in line comes from fear, but your inner cheerleader declares the truth with kindness: *You have done amazing things, and you are doing so well with all you have been through. You are okay where you are today, exactly as you are. You are strong and powerful.*

After speaking with Liz, I recommitted to showing up as the friend I needed most. The more I do this, the more I realize that my inner critic only makes me feel worse about myself, but my inner cheerleader encourages me to keep going and reminds me that I'm doing my best.

Another change I made was replacing the word *should* with *could*. Instead of saying "I should be doing more with my day," I intentionally switched to "I *could* be doing more with my day."

Because this was the reality: I *could* be doing more. We all could. But did I actually *want* to do more? I started asking myself this question: *Amy, what do you* want *to do? What do you feel like doing?* If the answer was, *I'm tired and I feel like resting instead of tackling my to-do list*, then I allowed myself the grace to accept that answer.

It's all too easy to fall into the trap of thinking that being hard on yourself is the way to succeed. But self-compassion doesn't make you weak; it actually makes you stronger. When researchers study people going through tough times, they consistently find that the ones who treat themselves with kindness and compassion bounce back faster and handle stress better than the ones who beat themselves up.[12] Studies also show that people who use self-compassion exercises daily feel happier and less depressed.[13] They even have lower inflammation and better immune system health.[14]

Looking back, I can see how self-compassion was essential to my success as an athlete—but I didn't start out that way. When I was competing in the 2014 Paralympic Games, I felt so much pressure to become the ultimate athlete that I became extremely hard on myself. I had suddenly become the face not only of our sport but also of much of the Winter Games. I was on cereal boxes and billboards, in TV commercials and magazines, and doing back-to-back TV interviews. Yet despite all this validation, I questioned if I deserved it. I felt like I still had a long way to go to become the athlete I wanted to be.

My inner world became a constant storm of self-criticism that strained not just my relationship with myself but also my relationship with Daniel. My obsessive focus on discipline and self-improvement hurt him and pushed him away. In my mind, I was trying to be the best

I could be, when, really, I'd become unhealthily fixated on eliminating every last flaw.

At one point, I had a breakdown during training. My foot wasn't moving the way I wanted it to, and I became obsessed with figuring out why. I'd been working in our shop around the clock with tools and mechanics trying to get my foot right, but it wasn't working, and it was driving me mad.

My coach saw me start to lose it and said, "Amy, you need to have a soft heart with yourself." Suddenly, I felt lighter. I realized how harsh I was being. This understanding completely changed how I approached training and competition from that point forward.

Funny how we have to be reminded at times to simply be kind to ourselves.

As I moved toward the Paralympics, every time I caught myself being hard on myself, I would think, *Amy, have a soft heart. You are doing the best you can.*

This not only helped me get through challenging moments but also released the pressure I was putting on myself and allowed me to enjoy the journey I was on (which was only the most amazing journey of my life!).

It's easy to fall into thc habit of beating yourself up for not doing enough or being enough. But we are humans, not machines. We need to be loving, open, and gentle with ourselves like we would for anyone we care for.

Your relationship with yourself is the longest relationship you'll have in your life. The more you nurture this relationship, the more supported you'll feel, and the more you can move toward your goals. It all begins with you.

Be gentle, tender, and understanding with yourself like you would a friend. You are doing the best you can, and that is good enough.

TOOL: GIVE YOURSELF THE GRACE YOU GIVE OTHERS

Give yourself the support and tenderness you need right now, instead of waiting for others to do it for you. When you extend compassion to yourself, you become healthier and more resilient, recovering from setbacks more quickly and keeping the clear mind you need to reach your goals. Here are six tips to give yourself grace at the times when you need it most:

1. Be the best friend you need right now.

When you catch yourself being self-critical, take a deep breath and think of a person you deeply love and care for.

Imagine that person coming to you with the exact problem you're currently dealing with, saying the same negative things you're saying to yourself: "I'm not good enough," "My body is horrible," "I'm such a screw-up."

How would you respond? Most likely, you'd feel compassion for their pain. You'd tell them, "You are beautiful. You are strong. You've been through a lot, and you're doing the best you can."

Now turn that compassion toward yourself. Give yourself those words of comfort and understanding. By doing so, you are relieving pressure and stress and giving yourself the care you need.

2. Stop saying *should*.

"I should be working out." "I should be doing more with my day."

No. Stop with the shoulds!

Stop being so critical of yourself.

Replace the word *should* with *could*.

"I could be working out," or "I could be doing more with my day."

Then ask yourself, *Do I* want *to do this thing?*

If you don't want to work out or fill your day up with chores, that's okay!

3. Ask yourself why.

Why do you feel this way? What have you been going through?

Ask good questions, and you'll get good answers. "What's wrong with me?" is not a good question because it has a negative judgment built into it. Instead, ask a neutral question such as "Why do I feel this way?" This question has a better chance of revealing what's actually going on for you.

Don't beat yourself up about your *why*. That ends today. Listen to the answer and allow it to be good enough.

4. Have mercy for yourself.

No one is always perfectly motivated or on top of their game. Everyone has ups and downs and reasons why they're feeling the way they do.

Mercy means understanding. When you understand why you feel or act the way you do, then you can have empathy for yourself. That's when you're able to say, "It's okay, you are doing the best you can with what you have." Or "You'll be motivated when you're feeling better. It's okay to rest for now."

5. Replace self-deprecations with self-celebrations.

That parrot on your shoulder telling you that you're not enough or you're not doing enough? It's time to shut it down, right now.

When was the last time you listed all that you have accomplished this week, this month, this year, or even today?

Try it!

Make a list of accomplishments, because I guarantee you have achieved more than you realize. Give yourself the credit any outside observer would give you.

Don't consider just major milestones but also more private or "smaller" achievements. Sometimes just getting out of bed in the morning when you've been facing a major challenge can be a big win.

6. Listen to your needs.

What are your heart and body telling you? If you're tired, you need to sleep. If you're hungry, you need to eat. If you're sad, you need to cry.

If you're lethargic, maybe you need to rest, go for a brisk walk, stretch, breathe, move, or do some other rejuvenating activity. Either way, your mind and your body are telling you something.

When you honor your needs, you build self-love, and that is the essence of grace.

—

Giving yourself grace isn't self-indulgence—it's wisdom. When you treat yourself with the same kindness you'd show to a close friend, you create the emotional foundation you need to truly thrive, no matter what life throws at you. By greeting your difficult moments with curiosity and compassion instead of judgment, you make it that much easier to find your footing after a setback. The happiest people aren't the ones who beat themselves up; they're the ones who refuse to abandon themselves, no matter what.

NINE

NEGATIVE AND NARROW-MINDED to *Open to New Perspectives*

IN THE DECADE I've spent giving talks about resilience, hundreds of people have asked me how I deal with chronic pain. The truth is, I *don't* deal with chronic pain—at least, I didn't used to.

This new injury changed that.

Had I been in pain before? Yes, plenty. But it had always been temporary or circumstantial. As soon as the circumstances changed, the pain did too. Walking in prosthetic legs isn't typically painful as long as they fit right. I would snowboard for hours, and my legs would feel fine except for some bruises here and there. I danced on two prosthetic legs seven hours a day, seven days a week for three months straight while on *Dancing with the Stars*. Although it wasn't easy and my legs felt sore, just like anyone's would, overall I was fine.

So when sufferers of chronic pain reached out to me asking for advice, I had no idea how to respond.

Experts define chronic pain as a constant discomfort that persists for more than three months. After the injury, that described my situation perfectly. The discomfort was relentless. My leg always burned or felt cold and numb. I often found myself retreating to my safe place—the bathtub—several times a day to help soothe the pain.

One day while I was in the bath, I found myself dwelling on the pain and frustration. *Why do I have to go through this?* I wondered. *Will this ever end? Am I stuck in this terrible situation forever?*

Then it dawned on me that there might be an upside I wasn't seeing. I was dealing with a kind of pain people were constantly asking me about but with which I'd never been able to help them. Was it possible this happened to me so that I could understand what they were going through?

Maybe experiencing chronic pain is equipping me to help people on a deeper level, I thought. Instantly, I felt better. The pain was still there, but I felt some emotional relief. I was going through an experience that would increase my empathy for sufferers of chronic pain—and learn how to help them. Maybe I could finally answer this really important question that people were always asking me.

This perspective lifted my spirits. It gave me a new way to make sense of my pain, even though it remained very difficult to endure. When I *reframed* my pain, it took on a whole new meaning.

For years, people have been saying to me, "Amy, you're so positive!" and "Amy, you're so optimistic!" But that's not quite right. What I am is a master reframer. Over the years, I've taught my brain to respond to challenging situations by looking at them in a productive way.

Reframing is a key element of my happiness and success. In fact, it just might be the most important one. I can reframe nearly any situation in a positive light.

For example, when my initial hospitalization and amputation happened at age nineteen, I could have spent a lot of time feeling sorry for myself and mourning the things I was losing or feared I would lose.

Did I do these things for a while? Yes—but then I got curious about what would happen if I thought about things a bit differently. I asked myself, *Did I survive so that I could help others who are struggling? Can my insights teach others not only how to survive but also how to thrive? Can I use what I'm going through to help others experience life more fully than they have ever imagined?*

That shift in thinking helped me embrace the situation I was in.

I also stopped saying, "I lost my legs." Instead, I started telling people, "I have two prosthetic legs." That subtle shift in emphasis let me focus on what I *had* versus what I had *lost*.

Here's another example: Throughout my years as a competitive snowboarder, I always hated cold, foggy, icy days. There were many mornings when I would wake up on a race day, jet-lagged and in a foreign country, look out the window, see these dismal weather conditions, and think, *Oh God, today is going to suck.* The thought of racing down a mountain at 60 mph on a sheet of ice shrouded in fog did not excite me. My mechanical ankles don't adapt to conditions like this the way biological legs do, and the sight of the fog and ice would fill me with fear and dread.

For the longest time I told myself, *I don't ride well in these conditions. I suck on days like this. I'm just going to be hanging on for dear life.*

Then one day I said it out loud to the wrong person: the US Paralympic snowboarding coach, Miah Wheeler. He responded, "Amy, instead of telling yourself you ride horribly on days like these, why don't you start telling yourself that you ride your best on days like these? What if you woke up, looked outside, and said, 'Yes! It's an icy, foggy, cold day. It's going to be a good day'?" That idea immediately shifted my thinking. I started practicing this mental reframe over and over again.

At first, I had to trick myself. It felt like my brain knew the truth: that the conditions were rough and that racing would suck. But I continued to tell it, *Yes, but I always do well in conditions like these!*

Over time, I trained my brain to believe that I actually do my best in the worst conditions. And guess what? Eventually, I did. Not only did I begin showing up with more confidence on those days but also I would show up ready to tackle the day while some of my competitors showed up dreading it.

Miah's suggestion helped me figure out the secret sauce to racing. I ended up having some of my best races on the worst days. When I practiced reframing in other situations, I became more and more convinced that reframing wasn't just the secret sauce to racing—it was the secret sauce to life.

Two people living through the same situation can have completely different experiences depending on the filters they're looking through. Our brains believe the stories we tell them, whether they're positive or negative, and the stories we decide to tell have a dramatic impact on our quality of life.

The beautiful thing is, we can change our stories anytime.

Reframing takes practice. You may not immediately believe any new perspective you choose. In some cases, you may even start out feeling like you're lying to yourself. But once your brain sees the wisdom of the new perspective, it will get on board.

When you reframe, you don't stop feeling negative emotions, and you don't sweep them under the rug. The secret is to refrain from sitting in that negative space for too long. Let yourself feel your emotions fully, then fully commit to the new perspective.

Here are a few examples of reframes you can use in daily life:

You're driving down the street going to work, and you have a nice warm cup of coffee in your lap. Suddenly, someone pulls out in front of you. You slam on your brakes. The coffee spills all over you and the dashboard. Your immediate reaction is to yell, curse, roll down the window, and give the person the finger.

We've all been there, right? Well, there is a beautiful space between the event happening and your reaction in which you have a lot of power. In that short pause, you get to choose how to interpret the event and how to respond to it. Your power lies in that pause.

You can assume that person is an uncaring jerk—or you can get curious about other possible reasons they cut you off. Maybe they just found out that their child is in the hospital, and they peeled out of the parking lot in a panic to get to them.

Wouldn't this explanation soften your reaction and drain your anger in an instant? I sure know it would for me.

Or maybe you have a presentation to give later today, but you wake up feeling groggy because you slept badly. Your first thought getting out of bed could be, *Ugh, today is going to be rough! I'm so tired. I'm just going to be surviving*. But what if you flip this story around and say, *I'm tired because I didn't sleep well, but being in this state makes me show up more real and authentic, and I always connect better with people when I feel this way.*

Reframing a situation changes everything.

Reframing isn't easy, believe me! But, like anything, the more you practice it, the easier it becomes. As you get into the habit of reframing, your brain will automatically begin to look for a new perspective the moment something negative happens.

You can reframe anything that happens to you, no matter how big or small. You can reframe a romantic breakup as an opportunity to learn more about yourself and explore single life. You can reframe a surgical scar from evidence of your brokenness to evidence of your body's extraordinary resilience. You could reframe the big ugly weight-bearing pillar in your condo as a cool, unique, industrial accent to the decor (as I once did!).

I'll never forget the time someone said to me, "Wow, you have been really unlucky in your life."

I nearly choked on my food! I replied, "Are you kidding me? I'm the luckiest person in the world! I had a less than 2 percent chance of surviving, and I *did*. My kidney was a rare perfect match, and I'm so healthy because I have it. I've done everything in my life that I set out to do. I've achieved financial success doing what I love and helping others. I'm not unlucky at all. I'm the luckiest person on earth!"

How is that for a reframe?

Change your perspective and you change your whole life.

I can say without a shadow of a doubt that reframing is what has gotten me to where I am today—where I have not just survived my hardest challenges but also accomplished extraordinary things.

Many people mistakenly think success comes from luck or *just being born that way.* No. The people who succeed and thrive are the ones who *reframe.* They view the negative events that befall them not as horrible failures that mean they should stop pursuing their goals but as opportunities to learn and grow. As my friend Hassan Khan put it, "The people who are able to thrive in this world have a special talent for converting life setbacks into future successes."[15]

Yes! Success hinges on reframing adversity to your advantage.

Reframing opens you up to new possibilities beyond the one you automatically assume to be true. As such, it's a key element to building resilience—a pillar to both surviving and thriving. This technique has helped me find light in my darkest moments and turn every obstacle into a stepping stone to success.

I invite you to become an expert reframer yourself. Train your mind to see setbacks through a new lens. I have no doubt it will not only help you survive some of your most challenging moments but also will unlock some of your most extraordinary ones.

TOOL: REFRAME TO SEE A NEW PERSPECTIVE

Reframing is the Allen wrench of your mental toolbox. (For those of you whose feet don't require the frequent use of an Allen wrench, it's one of the most universally useful and important tools. I always have one in my purse, just like I always have reframing in my mental toolbox.) Here are five ways to practice reframing any situation:

1. Claim the power of the pause.

Before you react to a seemingly negative event or interaction, pause and pay attention to the story you're telling yourself. This pause is your chance to reframe the situation in a productive way.

Remember, reframing isn't about suppressing negative feelings. It's about acknowledging them and then intentionally changing your mind about *what the situation means*. Your feelings are always valid. But you also have a choice in how you see and respond to situations, which will influence how you feel about them.

2. Question your assumptions.

When we go through an experience that evokes negative feelings, we often leap to conclusions that we then treat as facts, and this gets us stuck in a victim mindset.

Because there are so many possible explanations for just about every event, how can you be so sure your first assumptions are true?

Here's a quick rule of thumb about assumptions. You have three options: assume the worst, assume the best, or ask and get answers. If you're not in a position to ask, then which option do you think holds the most potential for your health and happiness?

Pay special attention to the assumptions you make about your own possibilities and limits. Do you assume that you are broken in some way? Do you assume that because of your past you can't live a full future? These are conjectures, not facts. You can believe you are limited due to your circumstances, or you can look for the unlimited possibilities *within* your circumstances. You choose.

3. Be mindful of the stories you tell yourself.

Your brain believes every story you tell it. Think, *I'm tired and suck today*, and your brain will go, *Okay! You're tired and will suck today.*

If instead you tell yourself, *I'm tired and not feeling my best, but I always end up doing great work even under these conditions*, your brain will go, *Okay! We are still going to have a productive day!*

Your words have the power to make or break your day—the power to push you forward or hold you back.

We spend more time talking to ourselves than to anyone else. *You* are the most influential person in your life. Instead of believing the stories you automatically tell yourself, start telling yourself stories that serve you. Your brain is always listening.

4. Seek different perspectives.

One great way to change your perspective is by welcoming input from others.

If you're going through something difficult, seek out others who've experienced similar situations. If you can't find someone in person, try books, audiobooks, podcasts, or YouTube videos. What new perspective might other people have that you haven't considered?

We all form assumptions based on our personal experiences. But how many other experiences are there out there? When you hear from people with different perspectives, you'll see there are plenty of ways to look at your challenges, including some you never imagined.

This is why I love to read, and it's also why I'm writing this book: to offer new perspectives that you may not have considered.

5. Focus on solutions.

Instead of dwelling on difficulty, put your energy into finding solutions. When I lost snowboard races, jealousy and frustration would sometimes creep in. But instead of letting those feelings spiral, I'd pause and shift my focus to gratitude for the competition. After all, tough opponents motivated me to work harder and become a better athlete.

Sometimes I would even thank my competitors for making me a better athlete. If I wasn't ready to say it out loud, I would at least say it to myself.

I'd walk away thinking, *What did I learn that can help me next time? How have I grown? What can I try?*

"Failure" is only a reason to stop if you choose to see it that way. I invite you to *fail forward* and use failure as a learning opportunity. Every time you struggle or make a mistake, you have two options: give up or learn from the challenge and come back stronger.

—

Ultimately, the stories we tell ourselves are the most important stories of all. They shape our days, weeks, years—our entire reality. Wouldn't you rather spend your days feeling good, creative, and productive as opposed to broken and defeated? The quality of your life comes down to the stories you choose to believe.

You are the captain of your ship, and your sails shift according to your command.

TEN

LOSS AND LACK to *Living Abundantly*

IN THE MIDST OF THE BACK-TO-BACK SURGERIES that followed my injuries, pain was the force that woke me up every morning. The first sensation I felt every day wasn't the softness of my blankets, the touch of sunlight on my skin, or the giddy anticipation of snowboarding but a leg racked with burning heat, bitter cold, or eerie numbness.

Waking up to pain meant waking up to panic. I'd run through a mental checklist of all the things I'd lost: I couldn't snowboard, I couldn't walk without crutches, and I couldn't even get around my own house without stumbling or bumping into things. I'd gone from being a professional Paralympic athlete to not even being able to stand.

My first thought upon waking was usually, *Oh God that hurts*, followed immediately by, *So much has been taken from me.*

Day after day for months on end, I felt like I was waking up into a nightmare I couldn't escape.

Then one morning when I woke up, instead of thinking, *Oh God that hurts*, I thought, *Holy crap, today is the twenty-first anniversary of my kidney transplant—and I'm still here.*

Twenty-one years ago, after battling meningitis and fighting for my life, my doctors had told me I needed a kidney transplant. At the time, the thought of undergoing a transplant right after losing my legs felt so unfair.

The local hospital offered classes about how to live with a transplant, but instead of alleviating my fears, they scared the heck out of me. In one class, they told us about all the side effects from the immunosuppressant drugs I'd have to be on for the rest of my life, such as gaining weight, growing hair in unwanted places, and getting a puffy moon face. As if that wasn't bad enough, the immune suppression meant that I wouldn't be able to travel as much as I wanted. The risk of getting colds, flus, infections, and even cancer would be much higher for me than for the average person.

All in all, life with a transplant sounded horrible, and I refused to have one. Instead, I went on dialysis and put off thinking about it as long as I could.

Still, we decided that my family members would all get tested to see if they were a match for kidney donation, just in case. No one matched—except for my dad.

"Your match is nearly perfect," the doctor told us. "Almost like twins. It's *incredibly* rare for a child and a parent to match so well."

For the next six months, my dad and I went through endless lab tests, X-rays, and genetic tests, and my dad started coming to transplant classes with me. I was still scared, but I realized that just because the medication had possible side effects didn't mean those side effects were all guaranteed to happen to me. *Maybe it will be okay*, I thought, and that simple thought changed everything.

From that moment on, I made a conscious decision to shift my thinking from dreading life with a transplant to embracing it. I hoped that if I accepted the kidney mentally, my body would accept it physically—a classic case of mind over matter.

When it came time for the surgery, there was one hiccup: My dad had three arteries to his kidney versus the more typical single artery. Normally they wouldn't perform a transplant on a unique kidney like this, but because it was the first surgery of its kind in the state of Nevada and there were students and teams from New York and UCLA there to assist, the surgeons decided to move forward. Thank God they did! The surgery was a success, and after four days in the hospital, my dad and I were able to go home.

The amount of medication they give you after a kidney transplant is shocking. I took about twenty pills a day. As much as I hated swallowing pills and especially ones with potentially negative side effects, I made a conscious choice to never think of the harm they could do. Instead, I chose to look at them as a blessing. I intentionally swallowed them with gratitude, thinking about how they were keeping me healthy and alive.

—

Now, lying in bed with my injured leg burning, I started to think about all the gifts my dad's kidney had given me over the years. It had gotten me on podiums where I won medals. It was with me as I danced on a TV show that was broadcast into the homes of millions of people. It allowed me to spend my entire adult life traveling and speaking on some of the largest stages in the world and to stand on the highest mountain peaks and snowboard down them.

I also reminded myself that my kidney had helped sustain me through my leg injury and all the surgeries that came with it, including six that were especially hard on it due to the IVP (intravenous pyelogram) dye they used when taking images of my arteries. Even with my body taking so many hits recently, my kidney was holding strong. It was keeping me alive and healthy no matter what came my way.

As I contemplated how lucky I was, a big soft warmth bloomed in my heart.

I took the deepest breath I'd taken in a long time. As I inhaled, a warm feeling of thankfulness, blessedness, and abundance filled my lungs. I felt this warmth spread through my veins until my entire body was filled with love, light, and deep appreciation for all that I had. I've since come to think of this as the Breath of Gratitude.

My kidney was such a gift; it was the gift of life itself, and it also taught me the gift of gratitude.

As I went about the rest of that twenty-first anniversary day, my leg was still uncomfortable, but my feelings of appreciation superseded the pain. Instead of constantly reminding myself of what I'd lost, I thought of how grateful I was for all that I had.

The more I did this throughout the day, the more I realized how much I had to be grateful for. My husband was so loving and sweet. My career was so fulfilling. We lived in the most beautiful place in the mountains. I kept thinking, *My life is full of so many wonderful things*. As I said a nonstop string of thank-yous (some out loud, some in my heart), I felt present and complete. There was no lack, only a celebration of abundance.

—

I've since learned that gratitude has some of the strongest scientific backing of any positive psychology practice we can do. Gratitude alleviates depression[16] and improves mental health.[17] It can lower your diastolic blood pressure[18] and reduce the levels of inflammatory biomarkers[19] in your blood.

Back when my dad gave me his kidney, kidney transplants lasted only nine years on average. I have now had this kidney for twenty-five years, and every day I have taken the medication with gratitude. I have no doubt that gratitude is the reason my kidney has stayed healthy and strong for so long.

Another amazing aspect of gratitude is its ability to cancel out negative emotions such as envy.[20] You can't feel gratitude and envy at the same time—it's impossible. That means the more gratitude you practice, the fewer negative emotions you feel.

UC Davis psychologist Robert Emmons, one of the world's leading experts in gratitude, says part of its magic is that it allows us to more fully inhabit the present moment.[21] Gratitude grounds us in what we have to appreciate in the here and now, instead of letting our minds wander off into judgments and comparisons.

I had moments after I initially lost my legs when I could have easily felt envy toward people who still had their legs. But in those moments, I was so grateful to be alive that it didn't even occur to me to compare myself to other people, worry about the future, or feel angry about all that I had lost.

But you don't need a near-death experience to feel the power of gratitude; you can summon it for everyday anxieties too.

On week four of *Dancing with the Stars*, my dance partner, Derek, and I were planning to do a surprise dance dedicated to my dad in honor of his kidney donation. During the commercial break before we went onstage, I felt incredibly nervous. I remember telling Derek, "I feel like I'm going to get really emotional out there. How am I going to do this? It's hard enough balancing on my feet, and now I'm going to be emotional while doing it!"

Derek put his hand on my heart, then asked me to put my hand on top of his.

"Tell me something you're grateful for in this moment," he said.

I told him I was grateful that my family was sitting in the audience.

Then he placed his other hand on top of mine and said, "Think of another thing you are grateful for."

I told him I was grateful for how healthy my kidney made me feel.

Next, I put my other hand on top of his, and I told Derek how grateful I was that I had him to help me share my gratitude for my dad and the gift he gave me.

Derek called this practice gratitude stacking. By stacking gratitude on top of gratitude, I started to replace the anxiety that was breaking me down with empowerment and confidence. By thinking of all the amazing things I had to be grateful for, I started to feel strong. That dance went on to be one of the most special ones we did on the show. In fact, people still come up to me to tell me how powerful it was for them to watch. Gratitude got me out of my head and into a state of pure presence where I could perform at the peak of my abilities—an experience I've since had countless more times.

—

What I learned on the twenty-first anniversary of my kidney transplant is that my life doesn't need to be perfect for me to be grateful for it. I can be in pain and also be deeply thankful for everything I have. Gratitude teaches us that we can go through trauma and grief, change and challenge, and simultaneously live the most fantastic, joyful, and fulfilled lives. Hardship and joy, loss and abundance, struggle and success—these things are not mutually exclusive. They can and do coexist.

I also realized that gratitude is a state of being that we can enter through practice. We don't have to wait around for something amazing to happen or for feelings of gratitude to wash over us spontaneously. The more you make a habit of appreciating what you have, the more your brain starts looking for things to appreciate. There's a reason we have sayings like "The more grateful you are, the more things you will have to be grateful for." It's because they're true!

That day, I vowed to make morning gratitude a daily practice. And I have kept that vow. Every morning, no matter what else is going on, I wake up and think about my kidney. That's all I have to do to put myself in a place of deep reverence for life. This practice orients me away from what is lacking and toward an appreciation for how much there is to celebrate and enjoy. I now know that I'm blessed even if I never walk again a day in my life.

Gratitude for my kidney pulled me out of despair when I felt like I was losing everything, and it can help you, too, no matter what type of adversity you face. When you fill yourself with the light of gratitude, there's no space for fear to dwell. You realize what's still possible instead of getting swept up in what might go wrong. And you inhabit the fullness of your life exactly as it is, one precious moment at a time.

TOOL: WEAVE GRATITUDE INTO YOUR DAY

When you make gratitude a daily practice, you leave no space for negative thoughts to take root. The more you train your brain to notice what's going right, the less it obsesses over what's going wrong. Here are two powerful ways to strengthen your gratitude practice:

1. Create a morning gratitude ritual.

Every morning when you wake up, before you get out of bed or check your phone, claim the day with gratitude. First, take five deep breaths and come into the present moment.

Next, think about one thing you are deeply grateful for: your health, your resilient body, a loved one, the pet snuggled beside you, or an activity that makes you feel alive. Choose anything that brings you warmth and joy.

Let yourself fully feel the emotions this brings you. Let those warm feelings grow and wash over you. Feel your heart expand.

Sit in this space of love, joy, and abundance for several minutes before you start your day.

2. Schedule moments of gratitude throughout the day.

Don't wait for gratitude to arise spontaneously; instead, be intentional about sprinkling gratitude throughout your day. Here are some ideas:

- Make a voice note to yourself every time you notice something you're grateful for. Listen to it at the end of the day or in a weekly session.
- Say a prayer of gratitude before every meal.
- Write down a bunch of things you're grateful for on little strips of paper and put them in a bowl. Pull one out and read it every day or even several times a day.
- Write down things you're grateful for on sticky notes, then stick them to mirrors, cabinets, steering wheels, and other places you look often.
- Most importantly, express your gratitude. If you're grateful to a person, tell them. Thank them. Do it often. Do it to people you're grateful for in passing or to people you're grateful to on a more sustained basis, like your parents or children. This helps you feel the gratitude yourself. Plus, gratitude is contagious. When you feel and express it, others will too.

—

Gratitude isn't just a nice idea; it's a superpower. When you choose gratitude, you choose strength. You choose resilience. You choose to bounce forward. Gratitude doesn't just change how you *see* your problems; it changes how they affect you. When gratitude becomes your default setting, feelings like despair, self-doubt, and jealousy dry up and wither away.

Part Two

FORWARD

ELEVEN

RESISTING CHANGE to *Thriving on It*

PRIOR TO THE 2019 INJURY, I had spent much of my career traveling to speak for large corporations. Between snowboarding and speaking, I lived on planes and in hotel rooms. As exhausting as it could be, I loved every bit of it.

When the injury hit, my team and I decided it was best to cancel the next four months of speeches, even though I had the upcoming spring season fully booked.

Up until that point, I'd never had to cancel a speech before. In my industry, you can't just skip work because you don't feel well. These brands rely on you to open or close their events. I'm often the highlight of a conference; sometimes companies promote me as their keynote speaker six months in advance, and they can't always find a replacement quickly. Canceling is a big deal, especially when tens of thousands of people are looking forward to hearing you speak. But this injury was major enough to justify putting some of my upcoming talks on hold.

I assumed I'd be up and walking again within six months, so I kept some of my talks that were scheduled further out. But as the first of those commitments approached, I was still neck-deep in pain and discomfort and still unable to wear my leg. Not wanting to cancel, I decided to make the best of it.

Before the injury, I loved striding onstage in my dress and three-inch heels, my head held high, feeling proud and tall. But now I didn't have a second leg to stand on. I couldn't wear the dresses I used to. And my pain was still bad enough that I couldn't even sit in a chair with my leg hanging down.

I decided to test a few options in my living room. First, I thought I could crutch onstage on one prosthetic leg, then sit in a chair. But sure enough, having my leg hanging while I sat was just too uncomfortable. I tested out several other options. Finally, after dragging a long wooden bench upstairs from our basement and sitting on it with my leg stretched out next to me, I'd found my solution. *Okay!* I thought. *The bench works!*

Luckily, my talks are all about overcoming obstacles. *I can use the bench as material for my speech!* I thought. What better way to show up in the midst of an obstacle than by sharing how I'm overcoming it?

So that's what I did.

The first speech was for a financial corporation hosting their national conference in Palm Springs. I used a wheelchair to get through the airport, crutched onto the plane, got a wheelchair to my ride, crutched through the resort, and showed up onstage the next morning with a bench to sit on.

This was what I considered a high-stakes talk—one where I was being paid a great sum to motivate and inspire a large audience. It usually also means I'm either the first or the last speaker the audience hears from, which makes it crucial for me to make a big impact. For this kind of talk, I always feel extra motivated to show up with confidence and put on a good show. But on this particular day, putting on that kind of show felt like a very tall order. I felt vulnerable and weak. I wanted to stride onto the stage in my three-inch heels like I used to. But I couldn't.

I decided to use the power of vulnerability to my advantage. I took a deep breath, looked out at the sea of faces, and said, "I'm sitting on this bench today because I can't stand for very long. In fact, I'm not sure if I'll ever be able to walk again."

My voice cracked as I explained how this moment of uncertainty was teaching me what it really meant to turn adversity to advantage. Up until that point, I'd always talked about the obstacles I'd faced when they were safely in the rearview mirror—never while I was still in the thick of it. I felt more raw, real, present, and emotional than I ever had in front of an audience.

That day, I got multiple standing ovations: one the moment I crutched onstage on one prosthetic leg, one in the middle of the talk when I showed a video from *Dancing with the Stars*, and one at the end as I closed with the line: "It's not about overcoming your obstacles, it's about using them and seeing what amazing places they might bring you."

I left that talk realizing that, yes, my life had changed, but I could change with it. I could continue giving speeches as long as I was okay getting through the airport, feeling a bit vulnerable, and sitting on a bench. So that's what I did.

Little did I know that this was the first of many pivots to come.

The next pivot may seem minor from the outside, but it was a game changer for me: I got a scooter.

After the talk in Palm Springs, I continued to follow through with my scheduled talks. For the first few months, Daniel, my mom, or my sister-in-law traveled with me. It was so much easier getting through airports with an extra hand and someone to push me in a wheelchair. But I wanted to be able to travel independently, so I searched online and ended up buying a cute little travel scooter that folds up and goes under the airplane seat. I'd show up to the airport, Daniel would take my scooter out of our Toyota, I'd throw my backpack on the handlebars, and then I'd zip through the airport, dragging my luggage behind me.

Oh, and by the way, the scooter goes really fast—and it's super fun! For years, I'd walked through miles of airports on two carbon-fiber legs. Now I had this fast little scooter to get me from the ticket counter to the gate in a matter of minutes. Although some people may have looked at me sitting on this scooter with one prosthetic leg and felt bad for me, I realized pretty quickly that the scooter wasn't a setback; it was an upgrade. Some people even started chasing me down in the airport asking me where they could get one!

For the rest of the year, I traveled like this between surgeries and speeches. I even flew to Barcelona with my scooter to give a talk and then back to California for another one. It was the solution I needed to get where I needed to go, on my own . . . and fast!

—

While my mom and I were at the speech in California, we got alerts on our phones moments before going onstage that the state was shutting down due to COVID-19. The organizers and I decided I should still speak, as hundreds of vineyard owners had shown up to hear me. Immediately after speaking, my mom and I headed home—and the world shut down.

Daniel was in Europe with a group of Adaptive Action Sports athletes when the pandemic started. We worried they wouldn't make it back to the US, but luckily, they were on the last plane out before the borders closed. Because they were coming from a foreign country, they were required to quarantine for a month. We rented a house for them near our home in the mountains, and my mom stayed with me. She and I woke up every morning and immediately turned on the news, our eyes wide as we watched one country after the next get hit by the virus. It felt surreal. Who would have ever thought the entire world would come to a screeching halt?

I had always felt secure in my job as a speaker because speakers aren't just hired in good times; we're also in high demand when a country or an economy goes through a major challenge. I used to say that nothing could take our industry away. "People need us in good times *and* in hard times!" I said. But the speaking industry was rocked by travel bans and the cessation of all live events. The degree and speed of this change were unprecedented.

Indeed, I've never heard the word *unprecedented* used so many times as it was during the pandemic. Every channel we turned on spoke about how unprecedented this situation was. There were days when it felt like the end of times. My mom and I even started using up old canned goods in the pantry because we were too scared to go to the grocery store. One night my mom made a meal of canned carrots and canned peas, and I thought, *This must be what the end of the world feels like.*

But after the initial months of shock wore off, I noticed that I stopped hearing the word *unprecedented* and started hearing the word *pivot*. It was becoming apparent that things weren't going to simply go back to normal. The world had changed dramatically, and if we wanted to survive, we had to change with it.

For many, the pandemic was horrible. People lost loved ones. Some lost entire families. Frontline workers and hospital staff were under a great deal of stress. Businesses completely shut down. The world was full of painful uncertainty and horrendous losses. My heart breaks for all the people who experienced the worst of it.

But there was another side to the pandemic, at least for me. For the past year, I had felt like I was in an *unprecedented* challenge with my injury, the rug having been pulled out from under me. I'd been forced to adapt in big ways. Now I was no longer alone in that: The entire world was going through it with me.

I also felt an unexpected sense of relief when the world closed down. With this injury, I had been feeling a bit of FOMO, or fear of missing out. It felt like my life was on pause while the rest of the world was moving forward. The shutdown put an end to that. Now I wasn't the only one missing out on life. We all were. And we were going through it together.

The shutdown also lifted some of the pressure I had felt for many years to constantly *go, go, go.* I always felt so much demand to keep showing up, stay relevant, get on bigger stages, make sure I was advancing my career, be visible, and attend public events. But when the world shut down and no more events or opportunities were happening—*poof!* Overnight, all that pressure was gone. What a relief.

When the whole world was slowed down, I felt more comfortable resting and recovering. The shutdown gave me space to breathe and time to rethink my life and how I wanted to live it. Remember everyone baking sourdough bread? I did it too. I even made a fun cooking series on Instagram with my dog, Huckleberry. What a hoot.

But it wasn't all sourdough and sunshine. My business was losing an incredible amount of money. If I'm not onstage speaking, I'm not making any money—and I wasn't onstage speaking.

Within three to five months after COVID hit, all my travel and in-person events for the year got canceled, many of them without any plan to reschedule.

This is when my team and I realized that if we wanted to continue making a living, we needed to figure out a way to pivot. We began strategizing daily about how to most effectively turn my previously very in-person business into a virtual one.

We jumped into gear and started brainstorming all the changes we would need to make to accomplish this transition. But before implementing any changes, we had to reckon with the big question: How many companies would even follow the shift to virtual? Were they still going to host conferences at all, or were they going to cancel them completely until the world opened up again? Sure, we had ideas but no real confidence they would work.

We started by reaching out to every company that had booked me for that year, letting them know that if they still wanted to hold their conference, they could do it virtually—and that I could still attend. Some companies canceled their events completely and hadn't even considered a virtual option, but some of them had the same mindset as us and were in the process of figuring out how to do it.

I threw myself so fully at this new opportunity that I told companies I was available for virtual speaking before I'd even tried to speak virtually or gotten the equipment to do it.

One of the companies decided to bite. I thought, *Okay, here we go!* I went all in, ordering a new laptop I would use only for speaking, professional-grade cameras that would shoot high-quality video, and a ring light. I transformed my reading room into a studio. I rearranged photos and strategically placed plants for ambiance, then built a tower on my desk consisting of an old wooden box and a stack of books to get my computer to the right height.

I knew people would be seeing me as a floating head on a screen, so I found creative ways to keep the audience engaged. I'd start each talk by asking where everyone was joining from and have them type their answers into the chat box. My goal was to deliver talks that felt just as warm and engaging as if we were all in the same room together.

Once I delivered one successful virtual speech, the speaking bureaus that book me with clients caught wind and began booking me for even more speeches. Before I knew it, I was doing more talks virtually than I'd ever done live. Because I didn't have to travel, I could sometimes do two a day. It was the only time in my career when I could be double booked and make it work. Sometimes I would have a speech for one company at 10:00 a.m. and another company at noon. I was speaking for audiences all around the world. Sometimes forty thousand people at a time would tune in. And I was speaking at all hours of the day. I would even wake up at 2:00 a.m., do my hair and makeup, turn on my ring light, and deliver a one-hour keynote to a company in China at 3:00 a.m.

Companies were inviting me to give talks about bouncing back. But *back* always felt wrong to me. Life happens. We can never go back to how things were. Circumstances change. When adversity knocks us down, we need to cover new ground, not retreat to our former position. I thought, *It's not about bouncing back. It's about bouncing forward.*

I watched in amazement as my virtual speeches first doubled and then tripled my income.

Because of this fast and vigorous pivot, the pandemic ended up being one of the best times in my career. I was now in a position to reach even more people around the world than before and to hit professional milestones using only a laptop, a stack of books, and my willingness to keep showing up.

I've since met many entrepreneurs who significantly increased their income through swift, effective pivots. For example, many small business owners in the food industry realized that if they didn't want to shut their restaurants down, they had to pivot to a takeout-based business as quickly as possible. It wasn't easy. Ma-and-pa shops had a hard time getting started with the necessary technology. But those who figured it out eventually thrived, especially with companies like Uber Eats stepping in. Some of these restaurants even found they could serve more people with a takeout model than a traditional sit-down model and tripled their income.

Even though I was thrilled to be among the people who pivoted and thrived, I was still physically struggling due to my leg. One thing I've learned is that people often assume that if you struggle, you aren't successful, or if you're successful, you can't be struggling. The truth is you can be both struggling and successful at the same time.

One major source of pain for me was the loss of snowboarding and the lack of other outlets for physical activity in my life. Thanks to the pandemic, we couldn't go to the gym, and all the ski resorts were closed. Because of my leg injury, I also struggled with not knowing if I would *ever* be able to do the things I loved again. What could ever replace the feeling I got from snowboarding? Would I ever compete again?

One day I was having a good cry in my guest room with the door closed and my computer on my lap. I had just finished a talk and felt so grateful but also so sad that I couldn't just walk out the door and go snowboarding.

I decided to reach out to a therapist. I shared with her all I was going through and all I felt I was losing. When I had finished, she asked if I could think of other activities that gave me the same sense of fulfillment and challenge as the activities I was afraid of losing.

"Maybe you don't need to do the same things," she said. "Maybe you can do new things but experience the same feelings."

I realized that just as I had done a major professional pivot, there were ways I could pivot in my personal life too.

In fact, I realized I'd been pivoting all along. When I was nineteen, I wanted to be a professional snowboarder. After I lost my legs, I kept the same goal: to be a professional snowboarder. I achieved this goal—I just had to adjust how I got there!

I started asking myself questions about why I liked snowboarding in the first place. What did snowboarding do for me? How did it make me feel?

Then I asked myself about other activities that might let me experience similar emotions. How could I experience the same feelings snowboarding gave me but through a different outlet?

That's how I created my value exercise.

First, I took out a pen and paper and drew a circle. Inside the circle I wrote all the things I loved doing that I felt I was losing, such as snowboarding, working out, competing, and even standing and speaking at in-person events.

Then I drew an outer circle where I wrote why I loved those things. For snowboarding, I wrote three reasons: 1. Snowboarding makes me feel free and strong. It's a physical outlet for me. 2. It connects me with nature. 3. It allows me to have fun and connect with friends and my community.

I then drew an even bigger outer circle and thought of things I *could* do that might bring me those same emotions or experiences.

As a potential pivot for snowboarding, I wrote "surfing." I'd tried surfing before and thought that I might be able to surf without my legs and still get the same feelings I got from snowboarding with my legs.

When it came to speaking, I noted that although it was true that due to COVID-19 and my injury, I couldn't stand on stages like I did before, I was still speaking and connecting with people virtually.

For competing, I realized that what I most loved about it was constantly working on my mindset and trying to perform at my best. I enjoyed hyperfocusing on my diet, sleep, and training. What could replace that? I realized I could have a similar experience with speaking. I could approach speaking like I did competition: with hyperfocus on things I could do to perform at my best—good sleep, good diet, and proper planning and preparation. I could channel nerves and excitement the same way. It was a different kind of performance but a similar quality of experience.

We all deal with loss and limitations. We all deal with changes we didn't want. We have a choice in these moments: We can either let those limits stop us or we can pivot and find new ways to achieve our goals.

Whether you're dealing with a career transition, financial challenges, an illness or injury, or simply want to start something new in your life, learning to pivot opens new doors. You never know when that unexpected detour will lead to your destiny.

TOOL: PIVOT TO REACH YOUR GOALS

When an unexpected challenge comes up, you don't need to give up on your dreams—you just need to find a new way to reach them. Besides, the path you originally mapped out was never set in stone; it was just your best guess based on the information you had at the time. Learning to let go of plan A and embrace plan B is one of the keys to resilience. Here are some ways to pivot when life forces you to scrap your original plan:

1. Stay committed to your goals, but be flexible in how you achieve them.

The most successful people are the most adaptable ones. When the world changes, they change with it.

Being flexible doesn't mean giving up on your goals—it means being open-minded about how you reach them. As my mom said when I lost my legs and yearned to snowboard again, "Put your goals in concrete but your plans in sand."

Success doesn't come from sticking rigidly to plans you made in the past but from adapting to circumstances as they change. Real breakthroughs happen when you let go of what you thought things were supposed to look like and lean in to *what is*.

2. Brainstorm alternative paths.

This value exercise helps you adapt to change by identifying what you loved about your old life and finding new ways to experience the things you most cherish.

Take a look at the following diagram:

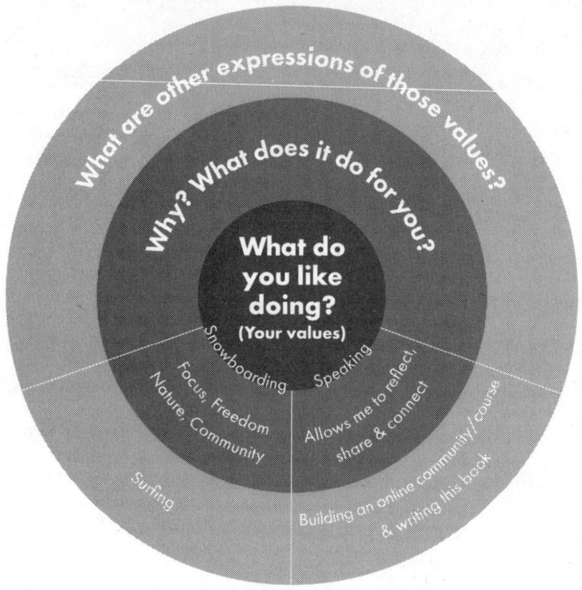

- Start in the center ring of the circle. What is it that you love doing but may no longer be able to do? In my case, the answer was snowboarding.
- In the middle ring, write what you love about that activity. I wrote about how snowboarding makes me feel strong and connects me with nature and my community. I could add: "Snowboarding challenges me." "It brings me freedom." "It makes my muscles work."
- In the outer ring, brainstorm other things you could do that might bring similar feelings or experiences into your life.

I wrote "surfing." In smaller print, I added: "Surfing helps me feel harmony with nature. I once felt happiness and freedom when I surfed with my legs. I may be able to have the same experience with my new leg situation."

After brainstorming possibilities, visualize yourself doing them. Feel the emotions these activities might bring, and let that excitement guide you.

When unexpected changes happen, it doesn't mean you need to abandon your goals or the activities you love. It just means that you need to adapt—you need to find new ways to express yourself or get the feelings you once had.

3. Commit fully.

Once you've come up with a creative way of reaching your goal, give yourself ninety days to commit fully to this alternative approach. Don't give up on it until the ninety days are up. After ninety days, if it doesn't work, then you *know.* Those ninety days will never be a waste, because I guarantee that during that time you will learn something about what *does* work, and that will get you closer to your goal.

—

Pivoting means redirecting your energy toward new possibilities instead of obsessing over the things that just aren't working anymore. Sometimes a pivot is a short detour and sometimes it's the path to a new life. Either way, when you embrace the pivot wholeheartedly, you don't just reach your destination—more often than not, you end up somewhere even better.

TWELVE

STUCK AND STAGNANT to *Creating Momentum*

DURING ALL THOSE MONTHS of surgeries and recovery, I couldn't move my body in the ways I wanted, and it drove me *crazy*. I'd gone from snowboarding six hours a day to barely being able to move at all.

To me, movement is freedom. In fact, I truly believe that movement saved my life after losing my legs. As soon as I got back on my feet, I started moving—and for the next twenty years, I never stopped.

I loved the sense of power and aliveness I felt when I moved my body. I craved the burn in my muscles, the surge of my heartbeat, and the touch of my breath moving deep into my lungs. When I wasn't training, I was riding a bike, hiking through the trees, or working out in my home gym. I think so much of my desire to keep moving comes from my grandma. At ninety-two years old, she is still moving, working out daily, and busy. I hope to be like her at that age.

I'd always appreciated the way that exercise benefited my mind. Whenever I was in a negative mood or stuck on a speech or problem, I'd jump on my spin bike, turn up the music, and pedal hard. Sweat would pour down my face, my mood would lift, and my mind would start to clear. It didn't fix everything, but it gave me what I needed in that moment: a little clarity, a little strength, and the momentum to keep going.

Momentum is that amazing feeling of being on a roll, whether you're working out regularly or showing up and working on your business every day. Suddenly, instead of feeling like you're the one working, it starts to feel like life is working for you. But the only way to experience this momentum is to take the first step.

When I moved my body, my mind and spirit followed. In fact, my whole *life* followed. So I stayed in constant motion.

To me, being forced to stay still felt like being locked in a prison.

And after my injury, I felt like I'd been handed a life sentence.

Most of the surgeries I underwent required two weeks of bed rest while I recovered, and some of them were much longer. I knew this was necessary for healing my delicate arteries, but I hated feeling my body get weaker and weaker. I'd sit on my couch and watch all the muscle I'd built over the years turn to mush. I practiced all the tools I've been sharing in this book to help me stay emotionally healthy, but the lack of movement made me feel mentally, physically, and emotionally trapped.

I remembered a time several years before my injury. It was just after New Year's, and I was going through an uncharacteristic period of inactivity. I'd set goals for the new year but was still recovering from Christmas; plus, I was at our home in the mountains, and we were buried under five feet of snow. I felt like I was hibernating.

Rest is important. I know that. But this wasn't rest; it was stagnation. I knew that because it didn't feel good. I wanted to do more with my days but couldn't find the energy. The days stayed dark. The cold hung on. Each afternoon, I'd melt into the warm embrace of the couch . . . and stay there for the rest of the night.

At the time, I wasn't just physically still; my life felt still too. There were no new projects on the horizon and no big speeches to prepare for. I wasn't moving, but honestly, there wasn't much to move for. Everything felt as still and frozen as the trees outside my window.

One day I got so sick of my lethargy that I forced myself to start moving. I told myself, *This is going to be worth it!* Then I pushed myself off the couch and went upstairs to my workout room. Once there, I stood on a mat and stretched for a bit.

Okay, I said to myself. *So far, so good. Keep going!*

I walked over to the speaker, turned on my music, and forced myself to get on the spin bike and start pedaling. As soon as I did, my mind felt clear, my energy bumped up, and I felt so much better. Before long, creative ideas started pouring into my mind. When I completed that workout, drenched in sweat, breathing heavily, and feeling great, I committed to moving more.

Every time I forced myself to move when I didn't want to, I would feel my mood lift, and I'd get excited about life again. After just ten minutes, my mind, body, and soul felt light and refreshed.

This is just one example of how physical movement creates momentum in every area of my life. It never fails. When I move my body, my mind gets inspired, my motivation grows, and my creative juices begin to flow. Somehow even my phone starts ringing more. It's as if moving my body puts my entire life in motion.

I'm a big believer in the power of energy, especially the energy we put into the world. When we're not moving—when we feel stuck and stagnant—our internal energy becomes sluggish and motionless too. But the moment you get energy flowing through your body, mind, heart, and soul, the energy around you starts changing too.

Energy wants to flow. Sometimes we just have to give it a little nudge.

When I was on *Dancing with the Stars*, my dance partner, Derek, said something that's always stuck with me: "Emotion doesn't create motion; it's the other way around: Motion creates *emotion*."

In other words, most people think that your mood dictates your actions: If you feel energized, you'll work out, and if you feel motivated, you'll tackle a project. But according to Derek, we can't just sit around waiting for the right mood to do things. We need to take action first and let the energy we need come alive in us.

If you find yourself having a hard time moving, even just changing your posture can make a difference. Are you slouching? When your shoulders are rolled in, you may feel small, and this can begin to collapse your spirit—literally. Rolling your shoulders back and holding your chin up high can help your energy and spirit expand outward.

One of my dearest friends, social psychologist Dr. Amy Cuddy, has one of the most popular TED Talks in the world.[22] In it, she shares her research about the connection between body language and mood. She found that the body and mind form a feedback loop: Stand strong and proud, and you will start to *feel* strong and proud.

Body language doesn't just communicate something to the people around you; it communicates back to yourself. When you choose expansive movements and postures, you're telling your mind that you *are* expansive. Amy's research confirms this: How you hold and move your body affects your mind, body, and spirit.

I've always instinctively known this to be true. When I move my body in a more expansive way, I begin to feel lighter and more inspired.

As I lay on the couch recovering from my surgeries, I remembered all that I knew about the power of movement. Even though I felt trapped by my physical limitations, I took every opportunity I could to move anyway.

Some days I would go upstairs to my workout room. Just getting there was a challenge, because it meant scooting up a flight of stairs on my butt. Because I didn't have my leg on, I would either sit on the floor or on my knees. I would turn on music and move any way that I could.

Turning on music made it *so easy* to move! I would play a song that inspired me, like "Dog Days Are Over" by Florence and the Machine (fun fact: This was the song Daniel and I played at our wedding as we walked down the aisle after the ceremony). I would do squats on my knees or sit-ups or push-ups. Or I would simply lift my arms over my head and dance, even if my lower body was sitting in one place. Without fail, by the end of the song, I would feel so much better. I would find myself thinking about new projects or things I wanted to start doing, like playing the piano again.

Movement does more for you than just build your muscles. It boosts your physical health, emotional health, and motivation to keep going no matter where you're starting from. The biochemistry behind this is remarkable.

Exercise floods your system with endorphins—natural painkillers that are so good at making us feel better, they often outcompete painkillers in studies. When you walk, swim, dance, or play, your heart pumps harder, energizing your body and boosting circulation. Your breathing deepens, delivering fresh oxygen to your blood and brain. The benefits are astounding: sharper memory and cognition, protection against cognitive decline, and improved mood. In fact, exercise consistently matches or beats pharmaceutical treatments for depression.

And then there's the biology of motivation itself. Dopamine is often called the reward molecule because we get bursts of dopamine when we expect something good or pleasurable to happen. Dopamine is what motivates us to seek out rewarding experiences—or, at least, experiences we *expect* to be rewarding.

When you move, your body produces dopamine. In other words, movement literally gives you the motivation you need to keep going.

Movement also helps you process trauma—physical, mental, or emotional. This is why somatic therapy can be so healing for so many.

My friend David Sutcliffe, a somatic therapist, once explained to me that trauma creates chronic holding patterns in the body. Our muscles tense, blocking natural movement and energy flow. Although this tension initially protects us, it becomes harmful over time. Somatic therapy guides you to move and to feel more intentionally, allowing old trauma to move through you. This process resets the nervous system. He likes to say, "It's only through the body that we can free the mind."

If I've learned anything from living the contrast between constant motion as an athlete and forced stillness after my injury, it's that Derek was right: Motion comes first, and emotion comes later. We often wait for motivation to strike, for healing to happen, for readiness to arrive. But those feelings show up *after* we set them in motion by taking the first step.

So if you're feeling stuck in your body or your life, don't wait for the energy to come to you. Instead, *be* the energy. When you move your body, you move your whole life.

TOOL: MOVE YOUR BODY TO MOVE YOUR LIFE

When you feel stuck emotionally or psychologically, the fastest way to shift your energy is to move. Your body and mind are deeply connected, so when you change what's happening in your body, you automatically change what's happening in your head. Physical movement can dislodge you from a mental rut and lift you out of a low mood—no thinking required. Here are some ways to use physical movement to create momentum in your life:

1. Start where you are.

Wherever you are, and whatever condition your body is in, start moving within your comfort level. Even if you're injured or can't move much of your body, move the parts you can.

You can start with wrist circles, arm circles, stretching, yoga, tai chi, slow dance, playing with pets, walking, getting in your car, running errands, going grocery shopping, doing chores, or going for a drive.

If you can't physically move at all, simply visualize yourself in motion. Amy Cuddy once told me that her research on posture and movement applies equally to people with major disabilities. A woman with quadriplegia once wrote to Amy's research team saying she couldn't expand herself physically, but in her mind's eye she was big. This practice helped her. They did the study and confirmed it.[23]

2. Move throughout the day.

We live in a sedentary culture where many of us work from our computers or stare at our phones for hours. Even people who hit the gym regularly often spend the other twenty-three hours sitting. Notice what changes in your body and mind when you sprinkle small movement sessions throughout your day.

I keep five-pound weights by my couch and use them when I watch TV at night with Daniel. While writing this book, I've been alternating between sitting and standing at my kitchen counter. I like to squeeze in mini workouts throughout the day, even just five minutes at a time: some squats here, some push-ups there. No movement is too small. It all adds up.

3. Use your body to change your mind.

Follow Amy Cuddy's advice: If you want to feel empowered and confident, roll your shoulders back, sit or stand up tall, expand your posture, and put your hands over your head. In other words, make yourself big! Do this for two minutes, and it will boost your hormones to make you feel more confident.

Play with your body. Stay curious. See what different kinds of movement help invigorate you in different circumstances. Remember: You can't control everything, but staying in motion—even the tiniest amount—*this* you can control. The moment you get moving, your entire emotional state will change. Go for a brisk walk or a drive and see how fast you become unstuck.

—

Movement isn't just exercise; it's medicine for your mind, sustenance for your spirit, and the fastest way to go from a low-energy state to a higher one. Every motion you make sends a message to your brain that change is possible. Every stretch, every dance move, every walk around the block is you choosing momentum over stagnation. Your body is the most powerful tool you have for transformation, and it's always ready when you are.

THIRTEEN

UNINSPIRED to *Inspired*

By the autumn of 2021, as my injury lingered, melancholy became my daily companion. I had no idea when this ordeal would come to an end—if ever. In that fog of uncertainty, I forgot what it felt like to be excited, energized, and alive.

Looking back, I can see that I felt this way not only because of my injury but also because of the COVID-19 pandemic. At first, the shock of COVID energized the world because it threw us into chaos and forced us to find new ways to survive and thrive. Many people felt inspired to do things like pivot their business or make sourdough bread (or both, like I did).

In the early days of my injury, I was similarly energized: racing to find solutions, undergoing surgeries, and pursuing treatments. The adrenaline rush of the trauma fueled me to take action. But as my recovery stretched on with no clear end point, I hit a wall. COVID meant that we had no idea when the world would fully open or what it would look like when it did. The uncertainty left me feeling unmotivated and uninspired.

Amy Cuddy refers to this as postpandemic flux syndrome. She says that when chaos or tragedy first hits, your body produces adrenaline to get you through it. But if the difficult circumstance stretches on for too long, your energy gets depleted, and depression and anxiety can set in. She explains that humans are not made for extended periods of chaos and uncertainty, and that's why as COVID dragged on, many of us felt dragged down.[24]

As summer turned into fall, there was a long stretch when I had no surgeries scheduled but also hadn't healed enough to walk. There was nothing to get excited about—there wasn't even anything to get *stressed* about. I kept myself busy with work and virtual speeches; I practiced gratitude and leaned into the tools I share in this book to lift my mood. But beneath it all, there were long stretches when I felt low. A quiet melancholy settled over me like a cloud that wouldn't lift.

I'd never experienced clinical depression before. Sure, I'd had low moments, but this time felt different. The sadness didn't pass; it persisted. I wasn't inspired. I wasn't creating. And the hardest part? I didn't feel much of anything at all.

When I give talks, people often ask me how I've achieved various milestones. I always tell them the secret isn't discipline or willpower—it's inspiration.

Inspiration had always been the fuel that drove me forward. Every major achievement in my life started with a spark: the idea to design my first pair of snowboarding feet, the calling to write my first book and build a speaking business, and the passion to cofound an organization. Even launching my newsletter came from the inspiration to reach people who needed hope. Each time, inspiration didn't just make me feel good; it propelled me to act.

So you can imagine how distressing it felt when I suddenly found myself completely *uninspired.*

But then one day something shifted.

It was late September, one of the most beautiful times in Colorado. Every year when the leaves change, Daniel and I spend as much time as possible outside because the brightest colors may last only a few days before a wind strips the trees bare. Ever since I was a little girl, fall has always been my favorite season for exactly this reason. It's one of nature's most stunning displays, but if you blink you might miss it.

One day, knowing that the season wouldn't last long, Daniel and I decided to work outside on our laptops. It was a perfect fall day. The air was still warm, and the aspen trees that surrounded our home were starting to change from green to yellow. The yellow leaves were so pretty they looked like little gold coins in the sun.

I was in the middle of editing a speech when I paused and looked up. It hit me: *The trees are spectacular.* I was in absolute awe of the aspens, with all those gold coins flickering in the breeze. Instead of diving back into the speech, I paused and let myself breathe it all in. My eyes filled with tears—not from sadness but from the overwhelming *beauty*.

It felt like something inside me was coming alive. After feeling gray and dim for so long, my mind began to buzz with ideas again. The weight I'd been carrying melted away, replaced by waves of love, gratitude, and excitement. The world around me started shimmering with possibility, and I remembered that *this* is what it felt like to be myself.

I started thinking, *Yes, I'm going to write another book!* I grabbed the notebook in front of me and started scribbling down ideas for the very book you're reading. New speaking topics started pouring out of me, complete with rough outlines. A little while later, Daniel and I found ourselves brainstorming a fun new business idea.

It had been a long time since I'd felt this way. I realized in that very moment that I was *inspired!*

My good friend, life coach Susie Moore, once shared that to be inspired means to be in-spirit. "You're with spirit when you're inspired," she said.[25] And yes—that's exactly how it feels!

Sitting outside with my notebook full of ideas, I asked myself, *Why did this happen? What inspired me?* It had been a long time since I'd felt this kind of shift in energy.

Then the answer bubbled up: *Of course! It's the trees!*

As much as I'd always loved nature, it wasn't until this very moment that I realized what the fall colors really did for me. It felt like they changed my entire chemistry. Looking back, I realized the beauty of nature had been doing this for me my whole life. Whenever I encountered autumn leaves, it completely changed me.

This realization was so powerful that I put a note in my phone calendar: "September 27: The trees were their most beautiful, and I was my most inspired." Knowing the impact this had on me, I decided to block off this week on my calendar every single year going forward. I share a calendar with my management team so that we are all aware of speeches, flights, and events. From September 21 to October 5, every year, my calendar now says, "DO NOT BOOK ME. I'M IN THE TREES GETTING INSPIRED."

I have stuck to this ever since. In fact, over the years I've turned down many speeches and work opportunities that have come in during that window of time. It's worth missing out on money and opportunities to take in the beauty of nature because of what it does for me. It's so important for my mental health and productivity. It absolutely replenishes my soul.

I also know that once I get inspired, there's no stopping me.

That day out on the deck started a chain reaction. Before I knew it, I was moving from inspiration to action. Now that I had the fuel I needed to light me up, I was accomplishing things in one day that had been dragging out for months, if not years.

To me, the element of action is crucial for inspiration. On *Dancing with the Stars*, a judge, Len Goodman, said after one of my dances, "Amy, you inspire me so much. You inspire me to go do something—not sure what but *something*!"

Exactly.

People often mix up inspiration with motivation, but I see them as distinct forces. Inspiration is the spark that ignites motivation. You need to feel that flutter of inspiration first, *then* motivation kicks in.

So if you're ever feeling unmotivated, ask yourself, *When was the last time I felt truly inspired?* If you realize it's been too long, it's time to immerse yourself in the things that inspire you—whether that's good music, acts of kindness, or a forest of aspens in the fall—and spend time with the people who set your spirit alight.

TOOL: NOURISH YOUR SOUL

Although we all love when inspiration arises spontaneously, it's also something we can actively cultivate. Rather than sitting around waiting for lightning to strike, you can seek out inspiration in nature, art, and acts of kindness or courage, and you can surround yourself with people whose example gets you buzzing to follow your dreams. Here are my favorite ways to find inspiration:

1. Connect with nature.

Take a walk through the forest, sit by a river, or explore a national park. Nature's beauty and grandeur can lift us out of our everyday thoughts and remind us that greater things are possible.

2. Visit a new place.

Check out a new city or a different neighborhood or just sit in a different chair and listen to different music than you normally would. New sights, smells, and sounds can nudge us out of entrenched patterns and reconnect us with our innate creativity.

3. Dig in the dirt.

Gardening or farming can reignite your sense of awe. When you tend plants, you get to nurture life and see your ideas grow. Watching seeds germinate and flowers bloom reminds you that wonderful things spring from humble beginnings.

4. Volunteer.

Giving your time to serve reminds you of your power to make a difference. Nothing fuels inspiration like knowing you're part of something bigger than yourself.

5. Seek divine guidance.

Connecting with the divine reminds you that life is bigger than your immediate problems or circumstances and that you're not alone in your struggle. Whether it's through prayer, meditation, or gazing at the stars, tapping into a sense of profound wisdom and benevolence can restore your inspiration.

6. Surround yourself with inspired people.

Spend time with friends or mentors who are passionate, creative, and motivated. When you're around people who are having fun and thinking big, their enthusiasm is contagious, and you'll find yourself wanting to take bolder action and try new things.

7. Create an inspiration folder.

I have a folder on my phone labeled "Inspiration." Every time I see a passage, quote, or photo that inspires me, I put it in there so that I can look at it when I need inspiration.

You could also put these things on a vision board you look at daily or scrawl quotes on sticky notes you place on your mirror, steering wheel, computer monitor, refrigerator door, or anywhere else you look often.

8. Create an inspiration playlist.

When I was going through surgeries and recovery, I often listened to the song "Rise Up" by Andra Day. (Funny story: Before she became famous for that song, I spoke alongside her at an event for the Olympics, and I remember thinking, *Wow, this woman is going to go far!*) "Rise Up" makes me cry, but it also makes me feel empowered to take on whatever's in front of me.

Make yourself a playlist of songs that inspire you. When you listen to this playlist, let yourself move, sing, cry, and feel. Whatever the music does to you, allow it.

9. Put it on your calendar.

Inspiration is your soul telling you what it needs to feel alive. Be intentional about giving yourself these things on a regular basis. Can you set aside a few minutes a day to engage with something that inspires you? What about a few hours a week?

—

Don't wait for inspiration to find you; instead, cultivate it consciously. Weave it into your life in as many ways as you can. When you make inspiration an intentional part of your day, you'll continuously feed your creative spirit instead of letting it run dry. By surrounding yourself with the sights, sounds, and people who inspire you, your soul will have what it needs to soar.

FOURTEEN

LIMITED to *Limitless*

EVERY DAY WHILE RECOVERING from my surgeries, I would lie on the couch, close my eyes, and go for a run. In my mind's eye, I could see and feel it all with perfect clarity:

I'm running through my neighborhood and down the dirt road. I can feel my feet hit the ground and hear the gravel crunching under my shoes. I run through the trees, smelling the sweet pine needles and fresh grass. I run up the long driveway to our garage, then up and down the stairs.

I feel my heart pumping and my calves flexing. Blood is rushing through my veins all the way down to the very bottom of my leg as my muscles contract. The small vessels in my leg are getting bigger and stronger with every stride. My feet are warm, even though they don't exist anymore.

This visualization was so powerful that by the end of it, I often felt like I'd just gotten home from a run—and as far as my brain was concerned, I had.

I had first learned the transformational power of visualization twenty years before, when I lost both of my legs below the knees. I remember the moment so clearly: I was still in the hospital recovering from my amputations. It was nighttime, and my mom was sleeping in the chair next to me. The room was lit only by the flickering light from the TV. Gazing at the wall, I started to worry about what my future was going to look like. I wondered if I would ever walk comfortably again, travel like I'd always wanted to, or be able to do the one thing I felt most passionate about—snowboarding—ever again.

But then I asked myself what would soon become one of the most important questions of my life: *If my life were a book and I was the author, how would I want this story to go?*

As I began to daydream, the first thing that came to mind was a list of negatives: *I don't want people to feel sorry for me. I don't want people looking at me like a sad, disabled girl.*

Listing what I *didn't* want for my life was easy.

Next, I asked myself: *Okay, so what* do *I want?*

A series of images came into my mind: I saw myself walking gracefully. I saw myself helping other people, showing them that whatever challenges they were facing, everything was going to be okay. I saw myself snowboarding again.

I didn't just *see* myself snowboarding. I visualized it in such fine detail that I could actually *feel* it. I could feel the wind against my face and the beat of my racing heart as if the whole experience was happening in that very moment.

That night, I didn't know how I would do any of the things I was imagining. But I knew that somehow I would. This deep certainty was all I needed to start moving toward my goals, and eventually everything I saw that night in the hospital came true.

Visualization is the process of picturing something in your mind and imagining what it feels like to do it. Scientists sometimes call this mental rehearsal. When you rehearse an activity through visualization, your brain activates the same neural pathways it would if you were actually doing it. It begins rewiring itself as if the conditions you visualize are real, paving the way for your body to carry out these tasks in real life.

I know all this now. But back when I was nineteen, I stumbled onto visualization on my own. All I knew was that my brain would slip into a daydream so strong that I actually believed the things I was seeing could happen—and eventually they would.

Years later when I was competing as a snowboarder in the lead-up to the 2014 Paralympic Games, I started reading the book *Psycho-Cybernetics* by Maxwell Maltz.[26] Published in 1960, it was one of the first books written about how the brain doesn't distinguish between "real" practice and mental practice. Decades of research have since confirmed Maltz's early insights about visualization's power to train the brain.

When I first listened to this audiobook, I couldn't believe how much research there was to support a technique I'd stumbled across on my own. Every day when I listened to it while driving to the mountain to train, I'd think of new ways I could use visualization to help myself improve. It became a key ingredient to my successes both in snowboarding and in other aspects of life.

One moment in particular stands out to me.

It was 2014, and I was competing at a Paralympic trial in Slovenia—the last race before the Paralympic team would be announced. My performance would determine whether I made the cut.

The snow that day was wet and slushy. Instead of my board cutting a nice clean edge, it would push the loose snow around. It felt like snowboarding on marbles. The snow got so soft that race officials sprayed a salt mixture on the course to harden it, which only made things worse. The slush turned into crunchy ice that sent us slipping all over the course, hardly the ideal conditions for racing at your best.

One of the first features out of the start gate was something we called a Wu-Tang—an eight-foot jump so steep that it almost looked like a wall. You'd ride straight up on one side, hit a two-foot platform on top, then drop straight down the back. A second Wu-Tang was waiting right after the first one. In normal snow conditions, these features would have been challenging but manageable. The slush made them treacherous. The transitions disappeared, making them jarring and unpredictable, especially with prosthetic legs. The wet snow would suddenly grab our boards and slam us down.

During practice, I kept running into two issues: Either I couldn't pull out of the start gate hard enough to get over the first Wu-Tang or I would pull *too* hard, launch over it, and drop eight feet, landing flat on the backside. Because my prosthetic ankles don't bend the way biological ankles do, I would land in the flats and shoot off the side of the course.

I had never struggled so hard on a course in my entire career as a snowboarder. At one point, I threw my board down, went into the forest, and screamed in frustration. This race was going to determine whether or not I would become a Paralympian, and I couldn't even get over the first feature. This was our only day to practice, and I didn't even get a chance to practice the rest of the course. At the end of the day, I walked to my room in tears, feeling a horrible mixture of exhaustion, defeat, and panic.

After I shut the door behind me, I took a deep breath. Even though I'd run out of time to practice on the course itself, I could still do plenty of visualization. In a sport like snowboarding, you can only take so many runs. So if you want to continue to practice a course—and I did—you have to get *really* good at mental rehearsal while off the snow.

I sat in a chair and closed my eyes. I visualized different ways I could approach the Wu-Tang. Some of my ideas didn't seem like they would work. In my mind, I would see myself falling or catching an edge. But then an image of Daniel riding his skateboard at the skate park flashed into my mind. I realized there was a big bowl he used to skate that had a similar steepness to the Wu-Tang on my course.

I visualized the way Daniel would ride up the wall, pause at the top, then drop back in. I replayed his every movement frame by frame. Very quickly, I realized that the pause at the top was key to regaining control. I began inserting that pause into my mental practice of riding the Wu-Tang. Instead of seeing myself pulling from the start gate and shooting over the feature in one move, I visualized every detail: gripping the start gates, pulling out with my board flat, riding up the wall of the first Wu-Tang, pausing at the top like Daniel did on his skateboard, and finally dropping down the backside and into the second Wu-Tang.

That night, I mentally rehearsed this sequence over and over until it felt achievable. I had it down so perfectly in my mind that I knew exactly how I would approach it in the race.

The next morning, I was the first athlete to kick off the race. Instead of obsessing over everything that had gone wrong the day before, I focused on the plan I'd mentally rehearsed. I put my hands on the start gate, pulled out with my board perfectly flat, rode up the wall, paused at the top, rode down the backside, and then did it again on the second Wu-Tang.

I nailed it!

When my body performed the exact motions I'd so carefully visualized the night before, it felt like the very stars had aligned.

That day, many of the other athletes struggled on that Wu-Tang, but even though I'd failed over and over during practice, I completed it perfectly. I ended up winning a World Cup silver medal and securing my spot on the very first US Paralympic Snowboard Team.

I have no doubt that it was the power of visualization that helped me get there.

From that point forward, I applied this same technique to everything I wanted to achieve. I used it on *Dancing with the Stars*, visualizing every dance move and how it would feel before stepping onto the floor. I use it for every speech I give. I visualize myself walking onstage, feeling confident, delivering my talk, and watching the audience rise to their feet in a standing ovation. Sure enough, nearly every talk I've given has ended with people jumping up in an eruption of tears and cheers, just like in my mental rehearsal.

Our brains are far more powerful than most of us realize. Researchers have found that visualization helps people achieve goals,[27] heal,[28] sleep better,[29] reduce stress,[30] and grow physically stronger. In fact, studies have shown[31] that people can actually gain muscle strength just from visualizing, because the brain activates the same neural pathways that control muscles and stimulate growth simply by *thinking* about engaging them.

That's why I spent so much time visualizing myself running while recovering from my most recent injury. Every day, I would lie there and imagine my muscles and blood vessels expanding and contracting, coaxing my body to follow suit. I would breathe heavily and literally begin to sweat as I imagined every detail of running up and down streets, dodging between trees, and navigating our neighborhood's many paths and trails. All the while, I focused intensely on the sensation of blood pumping to my calves and movement coursing through my muscles. By calling these sensations to mind as vividly as possible, I knew I was helping move my body in that direction.

I did all this with no guarantee that I would ever be able to run again. But I knew that every other time I'd visualized myself accomplishing something, I'd been able to achieve it.

I know visualization can be as powerful for you as it has been for me. Whether you're in the depths of a struggle or riding the high of a success, this practice can align your body, mind, and spirit in the direction you want to go. This practice costs nothing and can be done anywhere, yet it can completely transform your life. If you can see it and believe it, you can achieve it.

TOOL: VISUALIZE A LIFE BEYOND LIMITS

Visualization works for any goal, whether you know the exact steps to achieving it or not. When you picture your goal in detail, your brain begins to believe it's achievable and starts laying down the neural pathways that will guide you toward it. Here are five steps to mentally rehearse your success:

1. Find a quiet space with no distractions.

Turn off notifications and alarms and sit comfortably.

Close your eyes and take a few deep breaths to relax. If you prefer, you can keep your eyes open and gaze at a candle flame, out a window, or at another sight you find soothing.

Find a way to be restful with as few distractions as possible.

2. Choose a goal to focus on.

Next, choose a goal such as giving a speech, taking a college exam, speaking up to your boss, resolving a conflict with your spouse, completing your daily workout, perfecting a dance or other performance, or undergoing a successful medical procedure—nothing is off-limits.

Picture the whole experience moment by moment. See yourself in action and imagine the precise sensations you will feel and experience as you move through it. Remember, your brain doesn't know the difference between a lived event and a mental rehearsal. The more you can see and feel yourself achieving your goal, the more your brain believes you can.

3. Be as specific as possible about how your vision feels.

There are two main ways to visualize: either from a bird's-eye view or in first person. When I visualized to prepare for snowboard races, I would use both a bird's-eye view and first person, switching between the two;

when I was on the couch visualizing myself running in the woods, I used a first-person perspective. There is no right way or wrong way, and both perspectives are useful.

Whichever point of view you use, the important thing is to home in on the details. What specific actions are you taking? What are you seeing, what are you feeling, and what are you hearing? What are you wearing? What are you accomplishing, and what does it feel like to accomplish it?

Let the powers of your imagination extend through your entire body—to your muscles, bones, and veins. Believe, even if just for one moment, that this future version of yourself is possible, even if you don't know how you'll get there.

4. Write about your goal as if you've already achieved it.

As a supplement to your mental rehearsals, try writing down a description of your goal as if you have already achieved it. For example, "I am so grateful I got promoted! It feels so good! My heart is fluttering with joy." Just as in visualization, be as detailed and specific as possible in your description.

Put your description in a place where you will see it often, such as a vision board, and use it to remind yourself of what you are working toward.

5. Carry the energy forward.

Once you've finished your visualization session, carry the sense of excitement and accomplishment with you throughout the day. Let the person you want to be in the future guide the decisions you make today.

—

Whether you're navigating tough times or pursuing ambitious goals, visualization is one of the most powerful tools you can use to get where you want to be. Your brain needs to believe in the possibility before it can create the reality. When you imagine your success in detail, you're not just hoping for it to happen—you're paving the way.

If you can see it, believe it, and feel it in your heart and soul, then you can achieve it.

To download my visualization meditation, scan the QR code at the end of the book, which will take you to resources that will guide you through this practice.

FIFTEEN

DREAMING to *Co-Creating*

TOWARD THE END OF 2020, I began noticing that the very bottom of my leg would hurt at night no matter which position I was sleeping in. Then one day I realized that all the nice cushion I had from the reconstruction surgery in Boston was gone. The bone was becoming more and more prominent. My heart sank.

With amputations and prosthetic legs, you need a good amount of muscle and tissue at the bottom of your leg to pad the bone. You don't ever want to put weight directly on the bottom of your limb in a prosthetic, but if you do, that padding provides crucial protection.

The whole point of the reconstructive surgery had been to shorten the bone, connect the muscles so that they would expand rather than atrophy, and create a nice cushion so that I could comfortably wear a prosthetic. But as the swelling subsided, I started to realize that I didn't have as much cushion as I needed.

Part of this may have been my fault. I'd asked Dr. Carty to take as little length off my leg as possible. Having plenty of length increased the degree of control I had with my prosthetic and allowed me to snowboard. I'd been nervous about taking too much off, so I asked him to be conservative. But now I was facing a daunting reality: I likely needed another surgery to bring my leg even shorter.

I jumped on a FaceTime with Dr. Carty and showed him my leg over the video feed, hoping we could avoid surgery. But he agreed that we needed to shorten my leg even more. Elective surgeries were on hold while the world remained neck-deep in COVID, but luckily this wouldn't be considered elective. We scheduled a second reconstructive amputation surgery for January 5, 2021.

The troops of Team Amy rallied to prepare. We decided Daniel would come with me for the surgery itself. Once I was out of the hospital, he would leave, and my mom would take over caring for me. I rented another apartment in the same building in Boston, which was starting to feel like a second home. I loved that everything would be close by for my mom. She had our favorite café downstairs, the grocery store across the street, and a Target next door—wonderful. For a plan made during the pandemic, everything fell into place surprisingly well.

The emotional preparation was much harder. I remember calling my friend Cathy Heller, a spiritual coach and thought leader. I told her I was approaching my breaking point. "I'm so tired, Cathy," I said. "I'm dreading another surgery."

"It sounds like you're being called for another divine download," she said.

What a delightful way to describe surgery—a divine download. Her words reminded me that every time I'd undergone surgery in the past, I felt close to God and the divine. In my most difficult moments, I always felt a deeper connection to something bigger than myself.

This reminder helped me feel emotionally prepared to go back under the knife. But just after Christmas, there was another blow: It became clear that my grandfather didn't have much time left to live.

I was close with Pops; all the grandkids were. I'm pretty sure he's the one who gave me my love of nature. I'll never forget all the time I spent fishing and camping with him and my grandma in the mountains of Utah.

Gene Campbell was an expert fisherman who collected vintage trucks, including his signature 1962 baby-blue Chevy. His plan was to give each of us a truck before he passed. The summer before, he'd decided he was ready. That was the moment we started to prepare for his death; we knew if Pops was giving us his trucks, it must mean he knew he wouldn't be around much longer.

Pops was eighty-nine years old, rode his bike a mile a day until he was eighty-seven, and was always gardening or doing yard work. He was as tan as could be, as he loved being in the sun, and was always healthy. He never needed medication, even though he drank cheap beer and ate extra-salted popcorn for lunch every day for over twenty years. He also hated going to the doctor. In fact, he often refused to go, and because of this, he had missed an opportunity to have hip surgery when he started to feel pain in his early seventies.

By the time he went to the doctor, they said that there was bone on bone and that the only fix would be a hip replacement, but by that point he was too old for the procedure. They told him he would just have to deal with the pain from that point forward.

Living in serious pain wasn't something he wanted to do. On a phone call just after Christmas, he said to me, "Amy, I am ready to go. Don't be sad. I've never been more ready in my life. I lived a full life and am ready to fly in the cosmos with Tesla."

My grandpa worked for thirty years at the Nevada Test Site as a project manager on some of their nuclear programs. He loved Nikola Tesla. He also loved the magic of the universe. He would listen to late-night talk shows on AM radio that would broadcast conversations about outer space, UFOs, and all the interesting phenomena that we can't see. It was all stuff I loved too.

When he gave me his truck, he said, "Amy, you have been the closest to the other side. When I pass, you should try to connect with me! I feel like you would be the one to do it."

I took that as a compliment. I'm not psychic, but my life is filled with magical coincidences. Daniel calls me a good witch. When a strange coincidence happens—like the time I told him I wanted to be on the cooking show we were watching on TV, and two days later I got an email from a producer asking me to be on that exact show—he'll say, "Well, that's because Amy's a witch! You just can't explain all the magic that happens in her life."

It's true. Magic does happen in my life, and Pops knew it.

When I hung up the phone, I knew Pops was ready to go. Pops never asked for help and never wanted it, but he was ready for hospice to come in so that he could finally rest. My family and I thought we had at least a few more weeks or months with him because he wasn't sick, but we knew that by accepting hospice, he was laying down his sword.

A few days after that phone call, I was giving Daniel a last-minute COVID haircut in the bathroom when my aunt Debbie called. Debbie was a nurse; she'd gone to my grandparents' home to help hospice settle in. She told us about how the hospice nurses were so gentle, compassionate, and kind with Pops. As soon as they arrived, they set up his room comfortably, helped him shower, and got him cozy in bed. They gave him a light dose of a painkiller and permission to relax. From that point forward, their plan was to show up daily and make sure he was still comfortable.

For the first time in his life, my grandpa let go of control.

"After he shut his eyes, he didn't open them again," Debbie said. "We don't know why he isn't waking up. The hospice nurses said the dose of painkiller should have been just enough to take the edge off; it shouldn't have put him to sleep. But over the last twelve hours, his vitals have slowed down."

She held the phone to his ear so that we could say our goodbye. It felt so sudden and unexpected even though we knew he was ready.

With tears welling in our eyes and dripping down our faces, Daniel and I said our goodbyes to Pops. I told him how much I loved him and how good of a grandfather he was to us. I reminded him of all the camping and fishing we did and told him I'd never forget how much he impacted my life. Daniel, who adored Pops, told him how much he loved him and thanked him for being in our lives.

When Daniel and I got off the phone, we hugged each other in tears.

Taking a deep breath, we left the hair-trimming supplies on the counter and walked out of the bathroom.

As soon as we stepped out of the bathroom, I noticed that the big ring light in my first-floor recording studio was on—I could see it glowing from the top of the stairs. I'd used the light earlier that day for a speech, but before heading upstairs to cut Daniel's hair, I'd asked him to turn it off.

"Babe, didn't you turn that off?" I asked.

"Yes, I turned it off before walking upstairs," Daniel replied.

"Well, obviously not, because it's on!" I said.

I hurried downstairs to turn it off. The light has a simple twist knob that clicks when it shuts off. I turned it until I heard the click.

When I rejoined Daniel upstairs a few moments later, I noticed it was on again.

Chills went down my spine. Pops had worked with electricity his whole life and always said that when he died, the first thing he was going to do was find Nikola Tesla. Right up until the day the hospice team arrived, he was reading a book about electricity.

Now the ring light had turned itself on twice since we'd said goodbye to Pops.

A few minutes later, Daniel and I went downstairs to make dinner. I turned the light off again, and as I settled onto the couch, I said, "Babe, what if that was Pops? He loves electricity. What if he's somehow turning this light on?"

We both were a bit spooked but also thought it was silly. We told ourselves maybe Daniel had just forgotten to turn it off the first time.

I sat facing the ring light across the room while Daniel started dinner in the kitchen. I was telling him about Pops's fascination with electricity when I said, "I wouldn't doubt that if he could come back, it would be through electricity."

The moment those words left my mouth, I saw the ring light turn on again.

I jumped up (on my one leg), and Daniel jumped back from the kitchen counter. We both yelled, "Oh. My. God. That's Pops!"

After an entire year of using that ring light for my speeches, it had never—not once—spontaneously turned itself on. And here it was on full blast, as bright as it could be! When I went over to it a third time, the knob was twisted all the way on to the highest setting. There was no way it could have turned to that setting by itself.

It has never turned itself on since.

That was my grandpa—at least, that's what I chose to believe.

The next day, Daniel and I woke up at the crack of dawn to fly to Boston. Pops hadn't yet passed, but he also wasn't waking up. It was difficult knowing I was leaving for surgery, but I also knew that my grandpa wanted nothing more than for me to walk comfortably again. We all agreed that it made sense to follow through.

After landing in Boston, we spent the day getting set up in the apartment. At 4:30 a.m. the next day, we headed to the hospital for my 5:00 a.m. check-in. On the way there, my mom called me. It was 2:30 a.m. her time. *Oh no*, I thought.

"Honey, I know you're checking in for surgery this morning, but I wanted to let you know that Pops just passed," she said.

My heart shattered. Sadness flooded through me like a broken dam. Daniel pulled into the parking lot, and we hugged each other and cried.

I thought, *This is the worst timing ever. I'm literally walking into surgery right now. I won't be able to talk to anyone or have Daniel or my family with me because of COVID restrictions. I'm going to be alone in surgery and alone with the grief of my grandfather passing.*

I cried and cried.

I felt so lonely, like I had a huge hole in my heart.

And yet after letting my tears flow, I got up and crutched myself into the hospital. I checked into surgery, they brought me into prep, and the surgical team and I discussed our plan.

Unfortunately, it wasn't much of a plan. The team still wasn't sure if they would amputate more of my leg or if they would just shave the bone down slightly. They wanted to get in there first to see what was going on. It felt strange going into surgery not knowing what my leg would look like when I came out. This time, I told Dr. Carty to do whatever he needed to make sure my leg had the cushion it required to let me walk comfortably in a prosthetic.

In the moments before I was brought into the operating room, I felt a huge wave of calm wash over me. I realized I was going under anesthesia within an hour of my grandpa passing. I thought, *I'm going to be the closest to him out of anyone.* I would be on the edge of death. Maybe I would see him there. As I was being wheeled into surgery, I began to feel sure that he was with me. It even occurred to me that he may have passed when he did so he *could* be with me.

Then I was out like a light. I awoke after the five-hour surgery without any idea of what had transpired but knowing one thing for sure: My leg didn't hurt. *Amazing!* I figured the painkillers must have been especially strong. The only discomfort I felt was a little ache in my hips.

A few hours later, Dr. Carty walked in. "We took off another three centimeters of bone and wrapped even more muscle around and under your leg," he explained. "We also took some fat from your hips and injected it around the bone to pad it as much as possible."

So that explained the ache!

For the following six days in the hospital, I never once felt pain in my leg. It was the strangest thing, as if my brain forgot to tell my body that it had just undergone surgery. Even when the nurses unwrapped my bandages to check the incision, which is usually painful, I didn't feel a thing. They would press around different spots to make sure everything was normal, but I didn't feel any tenderness or sensitivity. My leg was swollen and bruised, with a large incision at the bottom in the shape of a smiley face, but I felt none of it. I wasn't numb; my leg simply felt normal. I didn't even need an aspirin.

I was fascinated by this experience. My mind was filled with questions like *How does pain work? What role does the brain play? Was my grandfather with me? Did he have something to do with this? Was he making sure I wasn't in pain?* I don't know for sure if Pops was there helping me through this, but I choose to believe he was, wrapping me in his arms the way he always had.

—

I stayed in that hospital room alone for six days (Daniel wasn't allowed to visit due to COVID). I had the most beautiful corner room with huge windows, which let me watch stunning sunrises and sunsets every morning and night. Just like after my first Boston surgery, I spent most of my days gazing out those windows. I rarely picked up my phone and never turned the TV on; I just lay there gazing out the window.

As I looked out the windows, I felt so comforted and grateful—for the beauty of nature and the sunsets, for the fact that my leg didn't hurt, and because I believed my grandpa was with me.

I found myself daydreaming constantly, letting my brain wander wherever it wanted to go. Soon I started to feel energized and inspired. There were hardly any distractions. Because I didn't need medication, the nurses came in only during shift changes, leaving me alone for four hours at a time.

My friend Cathy had told me I was due for another divine download, and *wow* was she right. By letting myself daydream without distractions, my mind started connecting dots and thinking of things I normally wouldn't. *I didn't just need surgery*, I thought. *I needed a divine download—and this is it!*

The inspiration I felt was so powerful that I grabbed my computer and started writing down ideas. I decided right then and there that I was going to launch a podcast about resilience and all the things I was learning along the way. I would call it *Bouncing Forward.*

I called my social media manager to tell her I wanted to launch *Bouncing Forward* immediately. I had already scripted out multiple shows while sitting in my hospital bed. All I needed was a microphone.

At the end of those six days, Daniel met me out front of the hospital, helped me get into the car, and drove us to our little Boston apartment. My mom flew in the following day.

As soon as my mom arrived, I told her how inspired I was and that I was going to use this "downtime" to create a podcast: "All I need is a microphone, Mom!" It just so happened that right across the street was a guitar store that sold the exact microphone I needed, and next door was a computer shop where I got a cheap laptop I could record on.

Ready to go, I found the quietest place in the apartment, which was my closet. I scooted from my wheelchair to the floor, grabbed my new laptop and microphone, and pressed record.

Within days of leaving the hospital, I had my first podcast episode completed, the description of the show written, and the cover art finalized.

My surgery was January 5; *Bouncing Forward* launched January 21.

It's amazing what you can do when you are inspired to take action. You can truly make your daydreams become a reality.

—

I've always believed that we have a lot of control over our lives. We aren't just passengers on ships; we're the captains. But I've also always believed that we aren't sailing alone. God, the universe, the divine—whatever you want to call it—is our partner in life.

We are co-creators.

I do believe I'm responsible for making many of the events in my life happen. I've exerted incredible courage and effort to realize countless dreams.

But there have been so many things that are just too hard to explain. Sometimes an opportunity or a person appears in my life at just the right moment.

I call this magic. And importantly, that magic always comes after I put in the effort. It's as if I do my part—I get inspired, I take action, I do the work—and then the universe shows up and meets me.

A week before I launched *Bouncing Forward*, with my first two episodes already recorded, edited, and ready to release, I got three serendipitous emails: Tony Robbins wanted me to speak at one of his conferences, Amy Porterfield (a successful podcaster I already followed and admired) invited me to be a guest on her podcast, and bestselling author and top podcaster Mel Robbins texted me to meet up for lunch while in Boston.

Right then, I knew that I was hearing from all these people I looked up to because I was putting myself out there and shifting my energy. I love the saying "You don't attract what you want; you attract what you are." I was becoming the Amy Purdy who podcasts—and the universe was meeting me in an act of profound co-creation. I was manifesting a new reality for myself.

If you're not familiar with the term *manifestation*, let me explain. Manifesting is the belief that you can bring your desires into being by aligning your mental, physical, and emotional energy with the future you envision. So, by declaring myself a podcaster and acting as if my venture was already successful, I started attracting all these interactions with other podcasters and people who could help me.

Manifesting happens when you make yourself an energetic match to the things with which you want to align yourself. You change your beliefs and thoughts, which then changes your energy, which changes your outcomes and, ultimately, your life. By taking action on my dreams, I had opened myself to possibilities—which allowed them to come pouring in.

Right after its release, *Bouncing Forward* broke into the twenty most listened to podcasts in Apple's self-help and wellness category. To me, this was proof that we can do amazing things even during the hardest of times.

We can always make excuses to refrain from taking action. My excuse could have easily been that I was healing from major surgery. But I didn't even entertain that possibility for a second. Instead, I used my recovery time to get inspired, create a podcast, and put it into the world; then the universe met me there.

This is the power of manifestation.

This wasn't the first time I felt like I'd manifested something. For example, one night after I lost my legs, I visualized myself running on running blades. I didn't just *feel* that I would do it someday; I wholeheartedly *believed* it. I went into my parents' bedroom and told my mom, "Someday I'm going to run on running blades. I *know* it." The next day, I woke up to an email from a prosthetic manufacturer asking me if I wanted a pair of free running blades. Of course, the answer was *Yes!*

Another time, I called my manager about a company I'd never worked with before, telling him I wanted to reach out. He agreed it was a great fit. After the call, I opened my email, and the first message—which had arrived just minutes before—was from that exact company, reaching out to see if I would consider partnering with them.

Those are just two of many moments in my life that have been too perfect and magical to be coincidences.

But how? *How were these too-good-to-be-true moments happening?* I wanted to understand how this worked so that I could keep doing it. I grabbed a pen and paper and made a list of all these magical moments in my life, trying to see what they had in common. I discovered that every experience I manifested shared similar elements: visualization, excitement, seeing possibilities, and taking action.

Thanks to this reflection, I created the six steps to manifestation that appear at the end of this chapter—a road map to co-creation that I now invite you to use as well.

Sometimes you can manifest things quickly, like I did with my podcast, but sometimes it takes years. Often, the opportunity you receive is not what you initially planned. You frequently dream of something you *think* is the best path, but when you get there, it looks completely different from what you imagined and sometimes even better.

For example, growing up I wanted to be a professional snowboarder, see the world, and help other people. I got to do all those things—it just took losing my legs to get there. In the end, it turned out even better than I imagined!

—

I believe manifestation consists of one part effort and one part openness to magic.

When you get excited about an idea, you start cultivating the same kind of energy you would feel if that thing was already happening. This transforms you into an energetic match for the thing you want to manifest. Then, when you take action, you start bringing those dreams into reality.

The magic happens when the universe meets you halfway. Opportunities, coincidences, and signs appear, showing that you're on the right path. As you embrace these opportunities, your vision takes on momentum.

My good friend Johnny Schillereff, who founded Element Skateboards, always says, "The harder you work, the luckier you get." It's not one or the other—it's you and the divine coming together to make your dreams come true. That's manifesting: effort paired with an open heart.

Manifestation is a great example of science and spirit working together. In fact, I see these things as two sides of the same coin. I believe there are divine forces at play beyond our imagining, and this belief is not mutually exclusive with science. Science describes what's happening based on observations of the physical world. Spirituality explores what's happening beyond what we can see and touch. They don't rule each other out. In fact, they are deeply complementary.

One thing we know from the science side is that daydreaming is an important and often overlooked element of creativity. For me, it is the first and most important step of manifesting.

Although people often see daydreaming as a sign of laziness, it's actually a touchstone of creativity. Science shows that we daydream primarily using a network of brain regions known as the default mode network, which becomes most active when our minds are in wakeful rest.

During daydreaming, the default mode network connects with another network—the frontoparietal control network—which handles action and planning. While the default mode network meanders creatively, the frontoparietal control network focuses on execution. Together, this dynamic duo lets us envision future potential.

People who let themselves daydream on a regular basis show more connectivity between these two networks,[32] essentially strengthening their ability to turn dreams into reality.

In today's world, we spend so much time distracting ourselves on our phones. Some call it distraction addiction—we never let ourselves get bored. But what we lose when we swipe and scroll is precious time to daydream.

When we start putting in effort toward the future we imagine, our brains begin rewiring themselves to align us with our goals. Neuroscientist James Doty says manifestation is embedding an intention into your subconscious mind.[33] Manifestation means using not just your thoughts but also your senses and emotions to wire that intention into your brain and body. In other words, manifesting isn't just an art—it's a science.

But I also believe there's a spiritual side, partly because I've had many experiences you could call supernatural that prove to me there's a spirit world beyond what we see.

About a month before contracting meningococcal meningitis and nearly dying, one of my massage therapy clients told me my life was about to change dramatically. "You're going to cross over to the other side and be transformed," she said. "But don't be afraid when it happens."

A month later, as I lay in a coma in septic shock with widespread organ failure and a ruptured spleen, I had a near-death experience in which I saw the other side. I met three beings who communicated to me that I had a choice: to go with them or to return for a difficult but important and beautiful journey. I opted to return. If you read my first book, you know the whole story.

These are just some examples of experiences I've had where I felt I was rubbing elbows with the divine. I share them with you because these moments have given me a profound conviction: Love and divine energy are all around us and working for us.

Many people close themselves off to the wondrous possibilities the universe offers. But I have found that the more I open myself to this power that lies beyond me, the more I experience it working in my life.

Maybe you don't believe in the magic of the universe. I know it sounds woo-woo to a lot of people. It might to me, too, if I hadn't witnessed it working so powerfully in my own life. Or maybe you believe, as I do, that this is God's work—that divine energy flows through us all day, every day, though some of us are more aware of it than others.

Either way, I invite you to be open to co-creating with the divine. Don't just wait for it to do its work. Do your own work and meet it halfway.

TOOL: MANIFEST YOUR HEART'S DESIRE

The divine download I received in the hospital that week helped me manifest amazing things. Can I say that I have manifested every single thing I want in life? No—at least, not yet (otherwise, I would have twenty golden retrievers, a miniature donkey, and a property big enough to hold them all!). But I know that if I truly wanted those things enough to take action, it could happen. Here are six steps to making magical things happen in your life:

1. Daydream.

Give yourself time to daydream, whether it's sitting on your deck gazing at the horizon or staring out an airplane window. Leave your phone in your bag and let your thoughts meander. Don't try to direct your thoughts or set limits. Just let the ideas pour in.

When you let your brain wander, it can go to places you never could have expected, and when you release control and distractions, you connect ideas and thoughts in new ways.

2. Feel it.

As you are daydreaming, let yourself get excited about the possibilities. Let yourself feel the same emotions you would if you were living the daydream in real life.

For example, say you want to get in shape. Don't just imagine what you would look like; think about how it would *feel* to be so fit and healthy. Feel it as if it's already happening.

When I thought about my podcast in that hospital room, I got so excited because I was feeling the experience, even though I hadn't done it yet. That feeling is key to manifesting. It's what changes your brain and energy and brings those daydreams to life.

3. Learn.

Often, our dreams require us to learn new skills or fill gaps in our knowledge.

This can be as simple as googling information, reading instructions, or asking questions. Research how other people have accomplished the thing you're daydreaming about. Which steps did they take to reach their goals?

Educating yourself and building your skills are essential steps in manifesting the life you want.

4. Make a plan.

Once you've found the necessary information, start piecing together a plan. How will you live out your daydream? What are the steps? As they come to you, record them on paper, on your computer, or in a voice note. The key thing is to get them out of your head and into a tangible form.

5. Share.

Share your idea with someone or with several people. Speak it out loud to someone close to you who will be guaranteed to cheer you on. Tell your spouse or a friend what you want to do.

In all cases where I clearly manifested something, I had told at least one person what I wanted to do. By speaking your dreams out loud, you are not only putting them into the universe but also allowing those around you to conspire to help make those dreams become a reality.

6. Keep going.

Keep pursuing what you want and taking action toward your dream. Keep believing it's possible. You need to believe in your dreams to make them happen, and you need to believe you are worthy of attaining them. Keep believing, keep daydreaming, and keep taking action that aligns with what you want for your life. Only good things will come from it.

—

When you manifest, stay flexible. What the universe gives you in response to your dreaming might not always take the shape you originally thought. But it might be better. Part of manifestation is letting go of expectations and remaining open to possibilities.

Put in the effort, feel the excitement as if your vision is already happening, and make space for the divine to help your dreams come true.

SIXTEEN

DISCOURAGED to *Happy*

As I recovered from this second reconstructive amputation, my surgeon and doctors advised me to keep my leg warm. This would help with the burning discomfort and maximize blood flow, which was crucial for vascular injuries. This added to the long list of reasons my bathtub was my best friend on this journey.

By that point, I'd realized that surgeons are usually experts on one thing—and that's surgery. When I asked about other therapies that might help my leg heal or encourage my body to grow more blood vessels, even the most forward-thinking ones didn't have much else to offer.

Perhaps you're familiar with this: doctors who present the solutions they know but don't mention other options that could help you heal better, like nutrition or alternative modalities. I kept researching to see what else I could be doing to help my body along.

I knew I needed to learn more.

Even after the second reconstructive amputation, my situation was just as uncertain as it had been the day this all began. The blood vessels in my leg were functioning, but the trauma had left them extremely small. Plus, three big arteries typically feed the lower leg below the knee, but mine were either blocked or so small that they didn't even show up on blood flow tests.

All I had below the knee was a small spiderweb of capillaries too small to detect in an ultrasound. Even after all the surgeries, I was barely keeping my leg alive with a tiny trickle of blood. There was no way I could wear a prosthetic in this condition.

Around this time, Dave Asprey, founder of Bulletproof and often called the father of biohacking, invited me on his show, *The Human Upgrade*.[34] Biohacking is the practice of finding scientifically backed strategies to optimize health and performance. I'd always been fascinated by it. Some people are skeptical of biohacking because it doesn't always follow mainstream medical advice, but I was determined to figure out how to get more blood to my leg so that I could walk again. I thought I could pick Dave's brain about my situation.

We had an awesome chat about circulation, blood vessels, and the healing strategies I'd been investigating, areas Dave had studied extensively.

One strategy I was considering was hot/cold therapy—alternating between submerging your body in ice-cold water and warm water, starting and ending with ice-cold. This theoretically creates a pump effect in your vessels, forcing them to open and close, which strengthens them. Around this time, many of my athlete friends had begun using ice-related therapies inspired by Wim Hof, sometimes called the Iceman, who was gaining recognition for using ice therapy to improve many aspects of health, including circulation. But I was more focused on the hot/cold strategy for my blood vessels. Dave agreed it was worth a shot.

After the podcast, I called my surgeon to ask for his thoughts on it. He wasn't much of a fan because my leg was already cold. He worried that cold water might make my already constricted arteries contract even further.

"That being said, I'm all for you trying new things on your own so long as you're careful and have someone guiding you," he said.

"Hot/cold therapy contradicts what I'd normally recommend, but it's ultimately your choice."

I went for it.

I reached out to a Wim Hof therapy specialist to see how I could go about it safely. She recommended I start slowly to see how my body responded. She instructed me to draw the coldest bath possible and sit in it for two minutes, empty the tub, fill it with warm water and sit in it for two to three minutes, then cold again, then warm again. Cold, hot, cold, hot, cold, hot. She told me to finish with cold, as it would force my body to finish opening the blood vessels on its own.

I tried it at home, and it was horrible. Who wants to take an ice-cold bath? Sitting in the cold water covered in goose bumps from head to toe, my whole body screamed at me to get out and warm up. But I wasn't doing this for comfort; I was doing it for therapy. So I stuck it out, and I was proud. This is why they say ice baths build resilience. You can easily talk yourself out of sitting in ice water, but when you stick it out, you realize you can override your own thoughts—and that's empowering.

When I finished my first hot/cold session, my whole body was shivering. I wrapped myself in a towel and crawled into bed. About ten minutes later, I got up on crutches and noticed something incredible: For the first time in quite a while, my injured leg didn't burn or feel numb. It just felt normal. It also had a little pink color—the first time I'd seen that since before the injury in 2019. Usually after a bath, my "good" leg was pink or even red while the injured one stayed pale.

Fascinating!

The hot/cold experiment got me excited. I started thinking about what else I could do to help my blood vessels grow or expand. I'd been researching vascular science for a long time, but seeing real results motivated me to keep going. I thought, *What else can I DO?*

I started researching a word my surgeon had mentioned: *angiogenesis*. This term refers to the growth of blood vessels. Typically, arteries don't regrow. We have far fewer arteries than veins, and they lie deep in our bodies under tissue and muscle and along bone. They're positioned deep because they don't heal easily and need protection at all costs. Arteries bring blood to the limbs while veins bring it back to the heart. When you damage a major artery like the femoral or popliteal, as I did, blood flow to your limbs slows dramatically. Many people become amputees due to this type of arterial damage.

Angiogenesis occurs when the body is stimulated into making a new network of blood vessels. This new network doesn't mimic the old artery. Instead, it's a collateral artery: smaller, like a spiderweb, and a bit uncontrolled. Collateral arteries often form in small, odd, twisted shapes to do everything they can to bring blood to the area that needs it. In fact, some people with heart disease don't even know they have it because their bodies have created a collateral artery or system of miniature vessels that act as a natural bypass. This is the best-case scenario when you have an arterial blockage, and it doesn't always happen.

Some people make a lot of collateral arteries; some make none. Researchers aren't yet sure why. But everything that happens in the body is caused by *something*. I was determined to find out if I could stimulate my own angiogenesis. I had already decided smoking was a no-go, especially because of my kidney transplant. But there had to be other things I could try.

The most surprising thing I found when I researched angiogenesis was that it was typically considered a bad thing. Collateral arteries can feed cancerous tumors, so most doctors, such as Dr. William Li, bestselling author of *Eat to Beat Disease*, usually provide tips on how to avoid it.[35] But we're not all the same, and we don't have all the same health needs. For some of us, angiogenesis might be exactly what we need.

Although I researched and researched, I had a hard time finding ways to stimulate angiogenesis.

At that time, there was a social media platform called Clubhouse that featured chat rooms where conversations were held on different topics through voice only. One day, my friend Lewis Howes was hosting a chat room about health and wellness with about two thousand listeners, and he had a few different people on the panel, including Dr. Li.

Because Lewis knew me, I suspected that if I raised my hand, he'd invite me up on the panel; sure enough, he did. But rather than speak as an expert, I asked Dr. Li a question: "Dr. Li, I've read studies you've written about stopping angiogenesis in cancer patients, but I have a vascular injury and actually want to induce angiogenesis. Are there any studies on how to do that?"

He answered, "Believe it or not, research has shown that eating dried fruit can help promote the growth of new blood vessels. There's a compound in the skin of dried fruit that boosts angiogenesis."

I immediately left the chat, went into the kitchen, and gobbled down a bag of dried apples.

Over the next few weeks, I continued my hot/cold therapy and ate dried fruit while researching even more potential angiogenesis strategies.

Then one morning after doing my ice bath, I scooted down the stairs and got into the wheelchair I used to push myself around with one leg. I went to the kitchen, poured myself a cup of coffee, and noticed something:

I was *happy*.

It was the weirdest feeling. It struck me that I couldn't remember the last time I had felt genuinely happy. With all the struggle I had endured over the last few years, I had sort of forgotten what happiness felt like. Yes, I cultivated gratitude and felt inspired at times; yes, I cultivated presence in the here and now and felt productive at times; yes, I laughed at movies and loved on my husband and Huckleberry. But I cannot say that I had experienced a true feeling of *happiness* in the entire journey up to this point.

Yet as I sat there in my wheelchair pouring a cup of coffee, I was without a doubt happy.

How? Why? My life at this point still looked as it had for the last two years: seemingly unending surgeries, inability to walk, constant pain, and uncertainty about the health and future of my leg. I was still using a wheelchair to get around my house. I was scooting up all the stairs on my butt. I was still using crutches on one prosthetic leg to get onstage to speak. I was still in the same position. Yet suddenly, this morning in the kitchen, *I was happy.*

I realized the only thing that had changed was that I was busy solving problems.

I was busy researching and figuring out ways to help myself. I was taking action. I was doing my cold therapy in the bath. I was eating dried fruit. I was researching and talking to people. I was doing everything in my power to help myself. I had a clear purpose: to hack my own body and figure out the best things I could do to heal it.

I didn't have a guaranteed outcome. I didn't know if these therapies would work. I had some moments when my leg seemed to feel better or look a bit pinker than before, but I hadn't yet healed it. There was no proof that what I was doing was working. The happiness didn't come from an outcome. It came from simply taking action.

As I sat in the kitchen sipping my coffee and looking out into the snowy trees, I thought, *If the act of problem-solving is making me happy, then maybe we need problems in order to be happy.*

Maybe we are not happy in spite of our problems but *because* of them.

Wow.

The only way to problem-solve is to have *problems* to solve. As I reflected on this, I came to a conclusion I've never heard anyone else make: We need problems in order to be happy. Really. The process of solving problems gives us purpose and helps us feel empowered, and this elevates us into happiness.

When I say we need to solve problems to be happy, I know some people will raise their eyebrows. After all, some problems are incredibly difficult, painful, or even life-threatening. However, when you reflect on your life, I'm going to guess the most satisfying moments came from doing hard things and making it through. The process of doing hard things elevates our mood and gives us a sense of purpose.

There are two main ways people use the word *happy* in everyday life and in scientific literature. One concerns pleasure—owning things or having pleasurable experiences. Researchers call this *hedonic* happiness. The biochemistry is simple: You get a dopamine hit when you do a pleasurable thing.

But I believe that true happiness—the happiness that elevates us in mind, body, and spirit—is the kind of happiness researchers call *eudaimonic*, following Aristotle: the happiness that arises from a purpose-filled life. When you take actions that give you a sense of purpose and meaning, you increase your baseline levels of dopamine.

Authentic happiness requires a sense of purpose—and purpose is all about *doing*. Taking action keeps you in motion and elevates your mood.

Many of us labor under the illusion that a life of ease and convenience is the ultimate goal. But I believe the opposite is true. There's a world of difference between collapsing onto the sofa at the end of a long, hard workday and plopping down at 10:00 a.m. and staying for the next twelve hours. Rest is wonderful, but it can't be all we do. It needs to be folded into a life of action and purpose.

Achieving goals through effort can trigger the release of dopamine, and this may partly explain why we value the things we work hard for. If you had to put in a lot of sweat to make the team, you'll be more likely to feel a sense of pride and belonging that will drive you to keep working hard and value what you've achieved.

This is also part of the reason a home-cooked meal is often more satisfying than a delivered one, even if it's less tasty. Satisfaction comes from purposeful effort. It's not necessarily the result of a specific outcome—it's the result of *seeking* that outcome, which means getting busy, taking action, and solving problems. This is the formula for creating true happiness.

We often think happiness comes to those without problems and challenges, but what I've learned is the opposite: Having meaningful problems to solve can *spark* happiness. Problems give us purpose and drive, something to pursue and chase. They put us in motion, and that forward momentum transforms our lives.

TOOL: LEAN IN TO YOUR PROBLEM

Learning about and taking action on your problem gives you a sense of purpose and direction, with feelings of contentment and happiness as a natural side effect. Real satisfaction comes from trying your best, not from a life of ease. Here's how to build happiness by finding purpose in your problem:

1. Identify your problem.

What's standing in the way of your health or well-being? What's making you feel frustrated or stuck?

2. Mentally categorize this problem as solvable.

Even if the problem feels permanent or you've been told it's unchangeable, challenge that assumption. Is it absolutely true that this problem cannot be solved in any way?

3. Educate yourself.

Do the necessary research; leave no stone unturned. We often overlook solutions just because they fall outside the realm of things we already know. Like my friend Marie Forleo says, "Everything is figureoutable."[36] You just need to find the right resources to help you figure it out.

4. Take action.

Try things. Don't let fear of the unknown keep you stuck in patterns that aren't working. Experiment with new solutions, even if they're unconventional—just make sure to follow proper guidance to stay safe.

If something doesn't work, don't give up. Learn from the experience, then try something else.

—

The more you take action to tackle your problem, the more empowered and hopeful you will start to feel, even if you haven't found a solution yet.

As counterintuitive as it sounds, try to appreciate your problems for what they really are: opportunities. The most rewarding experiences in our lives often spring from the greatest challenges. Use each obstacle to grow your knowledge, strength, and spirit. You may discover that happiness arrives long *before* you reach your goal.

SEVENTEEN

GIVING UP to *Finding Your Way*

THERE WERE TIMES during my very long recovery when, even after using every mental tool I knew, I still had moments when I struggled to get out of bed.

Up until my injury, I'd always had a very specific and highly motivating reason to get out of bed: I needed to train. If I didn't train, my competition would beat me.

Now, not training, I often found myself lying in bed scrolling on my phone, feeling lethargic and useless. One morning, I realized the reason I felt so unmotivated was that I didn't know my purpose for getting out of bed anymore. I had lost my *why*.

Why get out of bed? I didn't know.

As I reflected on this, my mind wandered back to moments in my life when I'd felt exceptionally driven and even excited to get out of bed and start my day.

One moment in particular stood out.

In 2014, I competed in my first Paralympic Games in Sochi and won a bronze medal. I flew directly from there to Los Angeles to begin competing on *Dancing with the Stars*, which started just seventy-two hours after standing on the podium. I did *Dancing with the Stars* for almost three months. The day the show concluded, I went to New York and spent six weeks writing my first book. As soon as *that* was finished, I traveled across the country speaking with Oprah for her *Life You Want Tour*. I shot a Super Bowl commercial; I spoke on many large international stages; Daniel proposed, and two months later we got married.

My *why* was very clear: I was living my dreams and had to keep showing up for them.

As for snowboarding, I felt I'd accomplished all that an athlete could outside of winning a gold medal. I'd gone into the 2014 Paralympic Games as the face of our sport. I was on the front of a Kellogg's cereal box, on Coca-Cola cans, and on billboards. I had sports contracts with five of the largest brands in the world. I was on four commercials running at the same time. I was in magazines and on TV shows.

I had reached the pinnacle of recognition in my sport and built a significant platform. I decided to step away from the team going into the next season and focus on speaking and other projects. The plan was to return for a few 2016 competitions and see if I felt inspired to race again.

One of my first races back in 2016 was a World Cup race in Italy. One of my favorite things about World Cup racing is experiencing some of the most beautiful places in the world. We were in a small village in the Dolomites, and after taking a season off, I was excited to get into the start gates again in such a stunning location.

At the same time, I felt apprehensive. I'd had very little time to train leading into this race because I was juggling snowboarding with speaking events. I'd flown into Italy from a big speech and was scheduled to fly off to another immediately after racing. My bags were packed with both snowboard gear and business attire. Without my usual preparation, I felt less confident going in.

I remember getting into the start gates on practice day. The course was steep, and it featured a big icy wall at the start and a sharp heel-side turn immediately after. I watched the other women drop in with confidence and realized that although I had stepped away for a year and a half, they obviously hadn't. They were riding skillfully and with such confidence. They'd grown so much since the last time I had competed alongside them. When I stepped away in 2014, I'd had that confidence too. But now, with one foot in and one foot out, trying to decide if I even wanted to return to the circuit, I thought, *I'm the underdog here.*

Standing in the start gates, I was flooded with doubt. I started asking myself, *Why am I even here? Why am I even doing this?*

When the time came and I pulled out of the gate, I hit the jump, my toe caught an edge in the snow, and I slammed down hard. This initiated a pattern for the day. Over and over again, I slammed into the snow. I kept trying to make small adjustments to my toe edge, and I was just getting more and more frustrated.

The voice in my head that questioned what I was doing there got louder and louder. Every time I went back into the start gates to pull out again, I'd hear it say things like *I've already won a medal! I've already accomplished my athletic goals and then some. I have a life outside of this. I have a thriving speaking career! I don't even need to be here.*

Here I was getting so much attention off the slope because of my accomplishments, but I couldn't even get through a training run without face-planting.

I was embarrassed and exhausted. All I wanted to do was give up.

At the end of the day, I went back to the little hotel in the village and got straight into the bathtub (you know the drill by now). I called Daniel. "I don't think I belong here anymore," I told him. "I absolutely suck. Why am I even doing this?"

I felt completely and utterly defeated. Nothing Daniel said could help me. My mind was made up. I decided I would show up and race the next day. But if it went just as badly, I would throw in the towel.

I had just crawled into bed around 11:00 p.m. when the hotel room phone rang. It was the front desk. "Ms. Purdy," the attendant said, "there's someone here to see you."

I figured it was my coach. Who else would be here to see me so late at night? I put on my pajamas and headed downstairs.

As I rounded the corner approaching the bottom of the stairs, I saw a group of people standing clustered at the bottom. In front was a young girl, probably eighteen, in shorts and two prosthetic legs. Behind her was a group of adults, including a translator, who said, "Amy, this is Maria. We saw on Instagram that you were in the area. So Maria grabbed her mom, grandparents, prosthetist, and me, and we piled into the car and drove four hours hoping to find you."

I blinked.

"We knocked on every hotel door in the village," he continued, "asking if anyone knew where you were. We wanted to meet you because we wanted to know: How do you do it? How do you snowboard on two prosthetic legs?"

I was so impressed by that level of commitment to drive as far as they did and to knock on hotel doors until they found me at 11:00 p.m.! I was so happy they located me—that their trip was worthwhile after all. All these people in one car looking for me and not even sure they'd find me. *Wow.*

I went upstairs and grabbed my snowboarding legs, then spent the next hour in the hotel lobby showing the girl and her entourage how I snowboarded with them. I pointed out how I added wood to the heels to get onto my toe edge better and how I adjusted my ankles and the type of feet I was using. I also showed them how my legs were made so that they fit properly. It was amazing! Because the girl's prosthetist had come along, I was able to walk him through all the details of how I'd modified my legs for snowboarding.

Once we got through all the information, I gave them each a hug and told them to keep in touch if they had any other questions. Then I left to go to sleep.

As I headed up the stairs, I felt overcome with gratitude, humility, and appreciation. I paused midstep and took a deep breath as a sense of purpose washed over me. *This is why I'm here*, I thought. *This is why I continue to show up and compete. It doesn't matter if I win or lose. It doesn't matter if I'm the best in the world or winning medals. There are people who are looking up to me. Just by showing up, I'm telling them that they can show up too.*

Coming back to compete wasn't just about me, I realized. I'd been so exhausted and distraught all day, caught up in comparing myself to the other women. That was all ego—I didn't like the feeling of being an underdog.

But this experience was all I needed to help me see that there was a much bigger picture at play. *It wasn't about me.*

I lay down to sleep, full of awe at what had just happened. *This is why.*

For the next two years, I traveled the world towing a hundred pounds of luggage through airports as I competed in race after race, falling and failing over and over. This was all amid so many other struggles that came with working my way back up. And yet I never again, not once, asked myself, *Why am I here?*

Every morning when I woke up to train, I knew why I was doing it. When days got hard, I knew exactly *why* I wanted to keep going. When I got scared or overwhelmed, I knew *why* I was going to push through.

Knowing my *why* gave me all the drive I needed to keep showing up, even when times were tough and the path to success wasn't obvious.

I knew why I was there, and I was committed to it. No matter what happened, I found my way.

I ended up making the 2018 US Paralympic Snowboard Team and competing in my second Paralympic Games in PyeongChang, where I won both a bronze and a silver medal. At that time, along with my medal from the first Games, that made me the most medaled US Paralympic snowboarder in the history of our sport. I have no doubt that happened because I knew *why* I was there and was wholeheartedly committed to it.

Now, years later, as I lay in bed and reflected on the experience of meeting Maria, I remembered the way I'd been at her age.

I first fell in love with snowboarding when I was fifteen. I loved it because it made me feel free. While I was flying down the slope, I didn't think about anything else—not school, homework, or day-to-day worries. I was completely in the moment. I also loved nature, being in the trees and snow, having fun with my friends, and the feeling of my body working for me while I challenged myself. Snowboarding was how I found and expressed myself, and I knew it was something I would do for the rest of my life.

So when I lost my legs, I had a very powerful reason why I felt determined to snowboard again.

The doctors and even my prosthetist weren't exactly sure how I would do it. There weren't any prosthetic legs or feet out there that were designed for snowboarding or that moved in the right way. Yet before I left the hospital, I gave myself a goal: *I will snowboard again this season*. I hadn't yet missed a season of snowboarding, and I wasn't about to start.

I didn't know *how* I would snowboard on two prosthetic legs. But I was committed to finding a way, so I went on a mission to figure it out.

I started by going up to the mountains with my sister and getting on my snowboard with my basic walking feet. I quickly realized they weren't going to work. I was standing on my board trying to carve down when I tried to go onto my toe edge and realized that my ankles didn't bend like I needed them to. I lost control and shot straight down the slope. When I hit a bump, my legs detached from me and went flying down the mountain!

I was so embarrassed and discouraged. I thought, *Clearly, this is impossible!* But after the frustration passed, I thought, *If I can keep these legs attached and get my ankles to move the way I need them to, maybe I can do this again.*

That's when I first learned that the obstacles in our lives do one of two things: stop us in our tracks or force us to get creative.

I got creative.

I called every adaptive ski school across the country to see if they'd ever worked with a snowboarder with two prosthetic legs before. They all said no. They suggested I take my legs off and sit in a monoski (a single ski with a molded seat attached for people who have paralysis or can't use their legs). But I didn't want to sit in a monoski. First of all, I was a snowboarder, not a skier, and second, I *wanted* to use my legs. I wanted to snowboard on my own two feet. So I called and emailed every prosthetic manufacturer in the world and asked if they'd ever made feet for snowboarding. They also said no and repeated the advice that I should just sit in a monoski.

That's when I decided to make a pair of feet myself.

I knew the exact motion I needed, so my prosthetist and I put a bunch of random parts and pieces together. We took an ankle from one company and a foot from another. We turned the ankle backward, added some wood under the heel to help me get onto my toe edge, and kept it all together with neon-pink duct tape.

It was those feet that finally let me snowboard again. Those feet are now part of a display about athletic trailblazers at the Smithsonian Museum in Washington, DC—an enduring symbol of what's possible when you know your *why*.

—

I share these stories because they illuminate a crucial fact about my successes in life: When I found my *why*, I found my way. Knowing my *why* gave me a reason to get up in the morning and keep going no matter what came my way. When the going got tough, my *why* helped me stay committed. I consistently chose to get creative instead of giving up, and sure enough, my goals become reality.

Professor Angela Duckworth, author of *Grit: The Power of Passion and Perseverance*, argues that grit is the most important predictor of success.[37] Her research found that grit predicted success in a variety of populations, including Ivy League undergraduates, cadets at the United States Military Academy at West Point, and Scripps National Spelling Bee competitors.[38]

When you have grit, you do whatever it takes to get where you want to go. You demonstrate complete commitment to the process.

Looking back on my life, I realize that my major accomplishments—whether it was making my own snowboarding feet, going back to the Paralympic Games, starting Adaptive Action Sports with my husband, or competing on *Dancing with the Stars*—all started with knowing why I wanted to do them in the first place. I had a *why* that was meaningful enough to me that I knew I would find a way to do them.

I've also learned that commitment is key to making anything happen. When you are truly committed, you will always find a way. When you aren't committed, you will find an excuse—and believe me, there are plenty of those out there.

Challenges are everywhere. Obstacles litter every path. Will you find an excuse, or will you find your way? It's up to you.

—

If you're wondering, *But how do I find my way?* The answer is this: curiosity.

The word *curiosity* refers to a sense of wonder or interest. When you're curious, challenges aren't reasons to quit; they're opportunities to figure out why they're happening and what you could change to overcome them. In pursuing goals, curiosity means adapting and experimenting until you find the right *how* for your *why*.

Whenever I've committed to my *why* with curiosity, I've been able to overcome every obstacle.

One amazing example of this was on *Dancing with the Stars*.

Going on the show, I felt enormous pressure to present to the world what was possible on two prosthetic legs. People had never seen anything like this before, and I wanted to demonstrate just how capable I—and others like me—could be. But the reality was that dancing at that level was really difficult for me. I wasn't actually sure what I was capable of. My legs didn't move the way I wanted them to. I often struggled with the most basic moves because my feet simply weren't made for dancing.

But I was absolutely committed to going as far as I could on the show. I wasn't going to back down. This commitment forced me to find a way.

Every week, all the competitors would be assigned a new song and style, and we had to create a dance from scratch. My dance partner, Derek, and I quickly realized that my walking feet weren't moving the way I needed them to. As the other dancers were trying to figure out what kind of shoes to wear, I was trying to figure out what kind of *feet* to wear. Because there are no feet made for the cha-cha, or the salsa, or for any other dance that I know of, we had no choice but to get creative.

For example, there was a week when I needed to dance the Argentine tango. Tango requires you to point your toes. My feet didn't move that way. I could have given up but instead I thought, *There has to be a way!* I remembered seeing a pair of swimming feet in a magazine. The toes were pointed for flippers. I wondered if I could dance in those, and I called the company to ask. Unfortunately they said no because the feet weren't built to dance on. I called back the next day and said I would like to order them to swim in. And they sent them to us! Days later I was dancing on the very tips of my toes like a ballerina on TV for millions of viewers.

That is the power of commitment, curiosity, and not taking no for an answer! If the swimming feet hadn't worked, I'd have kept trying different options until I found something that did.

There were certainly times when Derek and I felt stuck and thought we would never figure it out. But I knew my *why* and was totally committed to it. My reason for being there was much bigger than me: to show the world what's possible and to be someone little kids with disabilities could look up to. I wanted them to see that if I could achieve my goals, they could too. When I committed to that *why*, I felt driven to explore possibilities no matter how tired or stuck I felt. Curiosity created the way forward.

That experience taught me this fundamental truth: If you find your *why*, the *how* will figure itself out.

So many of us want the *how* part figured out first. We want to know how to do something before we pursue it. But the *why* needs to come first. Your path may be filled with obstacles and unknowns, but you will be able to walk it and reach your goal because your *why* keeps you going.

—

After my injury, I realized I needed to find a new *why*—one that didn't hinge on athletic achievements or blazing new trails in sports. So what would it be?

I realized my new *why* was to inspire the people who looked up to me. So many people looked to me to give them strength through their challenges. I couldn't give up on myself because I didn't want all those people to give up on themselves.

That became enough of a *why* to get me up and moving even on some of my toughest days.

Sometimes resilience comes from knowing other people depend on you, and that's enough *why* to keep pressing forward. At least, that's what mine became.

Knowing your *why* may very well be the most important part of surviving and thriving. It is what motivates you to keep going on your journey, including through the often difficult creative processes that help you find your way. This is true for all things you want to do in life, from changing daily habits to achieving big dreams. Sometimes what you need is simply to feel motivated to get out of bed and go to work or to take the time and effort to prepare healthy meals. Whatever your goal, no matter how big or small, find and commit to your *why*.

TOOL: DISCOVER YOUR DEEPER PURPOSE

When you know your deepest *why*, you'll access the strength you need to push through any obstacle. And when you trust in your *why*, the *how* will begin to reveal itself one step at a time. Here's how to uncover your purpose and commit to it fully:

1. Dig deeper.

Ask yourself, *Why do I want to achieve this goal?* Then ask again. And again.

Don't settle for surface-level reasons like "I want this job because I want to make a lot of money" or "I want to be a professional athlete because I like sports."

Instead, dig deep and be specific. For example, "I want to make money so that I can become financially independent and my family doesn't have to worry about me" or "Sports make me feel confident and empowered. They help my mental health and show me what I'm capable of."

2. Commit to your *why*.

Once you know your deepest *why*, commit to making your goal happen, even if you're not sure how. You don't become an Olympian or a Paralympian with one foot in and one foot out. You get there by committing with your whole being.

If you're reluctant to commit, this is a sign that you haven't found your real *why*. In this case, go back to Step 1 and keep brainstorming.

3. Get curious.

When setbacks happen or you make "mistakes," don't beat yourself up. Instead, ask, *What can I learn from this?* and *What haven't I tried yet?* Curiosity keeps you focused on what's possible.

If your initial approach isn't working, try another one. You don't need any single method to be *the* solution. Curiosity means staying open to possibilities and trying new options until you find one that lets you move forward.

4. Get creative.

Brainstorm unconventional solutions. Test out counterintuitive methods. Combine elements that don't normally go together.

When your back is against the wall but you're committed to your goal, channel that pressure into innovation.

—

When you find your *why* and commit to it wholeheartedly, the things that would have held you back in the past no longer have the same power over you. Your *why* is like a beacon guiding you onward, even when the *how* takes time and effort to find. Fear, doubt, and outside opinions fade into background noise when you're firmly anchored to your purpose.

EIGHTEEN

RESISTANCE to *Acceptance*

AFTER THE SECOND REVISION AMPUTATION in Boston, my leg seemed to be healing just fine. I was grateful to have all these surgeries out of the way and to move forward with my life. Then one afternoon in late March, right before I was scheduled to jump online for a speech, my leg started feeling cold and numb. I put it out of my mind and followed through with my talk. After all, I was used to the ups and downs of healing.

But when my leg was still cold and numb the next day, I began to worry. It had been months since I'd felt something so out of the ordinary.

I called Dr. Mubarak, drove down to Denver, and got an ultrasound. The results crushed me.

My femoral and popliteal arteries had closed in the same area of the knee that had started this whole journey two years before. *Oh my God,* I thought. *This can't be happening.* I'd had nine surgeries over two years, including two additional leg amputations, all trying to save my leg and open this artery—and here I was back at square one.

My heart sank, and my head whirled with doubts. Had any of this been worth it?

"I can do one more angiogram to see what's going on," said Dr. Mubarak. "We can reassess from there."

As exhausted as I was from years of fighting, I knew I wasn't ready to give up. "Let's do it," I said.

A few days later, Dr. Mubarak did the angiogram. He saw where the artery had closed and successfully opened it up. Next, he checked the arteries below the knee. He expected them to be closed, as these arteries had been blocked and inoperable since the very beginning.

However, he found that the arteries were not as hard as concrete, as we had originally been told would happen. Even years later, they were surprisingly soft. This meant he could go in with tPA—the same clot buster Dr. Cooper had used two years before—and try to open everything up one last time.

"You have two options," he said. "Either we can leave things how they are, which means your arteries will stay closed, or I can go in and try to clear them out one last time."

I sighed. Exhaustion pressed down on me like a heavy weight. I'd been so sure the last surgery would be the final ordeal. How could I go through another procedure? But I also wasn't ready to give up after coming this far. *At this point*, I thought, *what do I have to lose?*

That evening, I had a long conversation with Daniel.

"I don't know about this," he said, his voice anguished. "Remember how excruciating the tPA drip was the first time you did it? I don't know if I can sit there and watch you go through that level of pain again."

"I know," I said. "But at least if I do this, I'll know I tried absolutely everything to save my leg. If it doesn't work, I'll feel better knowing I tried."

Daniel nodded. Ultimately, we agreed to go ahead with it.

Just weeks before, we'd purchased a condo in Denver so that we could have easy access to flights and prosthetic appointments. I'd been expecting to start working on a prosthetic leg soon, a process that can take months or even years to get right. We'd intentionally chosen a building that felt like a health resort. It had yoga classes, an infinity pool and sauna, and an organic garden covering most of the second floor, where gardeners harvested baskets of vegetables to give to residents each week. I was craving a healing environment for my recovery, and this was perfect.

On a Monday morning, we left our condo and headed to the hospital.

Dr. Mubarak brought me into the operating room, inserted the catheter into my femoral artery, started the tPA drip, and then moved me into a hospital room to wait. The procedure could last anywhere from one to three days depending on how quickly my artery cleared.

The first two hours weren't too painful, thanks to the morphine coming in through my IV. But in hour three, the pain shot up to an unbearable level. The nurses gave me every strong painkiller they had, but it didn't even take the edge off.

Every time Dr. Mubarak checked on me, he asked if I wanted to continue. I gritted my teeth and said yes. I wasn't ready to give up, even with the excruciating pain.

The next morning the team brought me back into the operating room to see how much of the blockage the tPA had dissolved. Thankfully, they found that it had cleared almost all the blockage in my thigh and below the knee.

For the next two weeks, I lay in bed recovering. My leg wasn't worse, but it also wasn't significantly better.

At the end of the two weeks, I went for an ultrasound. I'd had so many ultrasounds over the last few years that I'd gotten to know the technicians, and they always told me what they were seeing. But this time the tech was quiet. After finishing the test, she brought me into another room where Dr. Mubarak came in to meet me.

"How are you feeling?" he asked.

"Well, my leg burns and hurts, but it's warm, so I think what we did worked," I said. "If it feels warm, it means there's blood flow—right?"

"I'm happy it feels warm," he said, "because all the arteries have closed."

My jaw dropped. I looked at him in disbelief. "What?" I managed to say.

He said, "From the beginning, we knew we were just buying time and that eventually your arteries would close. We were hoping to buy even more time, but at this point there's nothing more I can do."

After all the pain and effort—all the surgeries—everything I'd gone through over the past two years to keep my arteries open, they had officially closed.

I sat in shock as I realized that I might have to lose the rest of my leg. But over the next few minutes as the initial shock wore off, I felt something unexpected: peace.

I'd spent the last two years fighting to keep my leg. I'd given it everything I had. Now that I'd run out of options, I realized just how much that fight had consumed me. It was time to lay down my sword and accept whatever came next.

As Daniel and I drove home from Dr. Mubarak's office, I broke the silence to say, "We did everything we could to save my leg. Now it's up to my body, God, and the universe to do their work. Whatever happens, I will accept it."

Throughout this journey, I'd had many moments where I *thought* I was surrendering, when deep down, I wasn't ready to hand over control.

This time was different. Even though my leg still hurt, I was flooded with relief. I knew I could finally stop fighting. It was no longer up to me or my surgeon if my leg recovered; it was out of our hands. Nothing felt better than to finally let go of that control.

As Daniel quietly navigated the Denver streets back to our condo, I remembered the near-death experience I'd had twenty years ago—the one where three beings gave me the choice to go with them or come back to Earth.

When I made the choice to come back, I remember seeing and feeling a bright warm light over my shoulder. I recall hearing, "Whatever you go through in life, just remember it will all make sense in the end."

That experience changed everything. When I woke up and realized I would lose my legs and my kidneys, I had something to hold on to. As uncertain as I felt at times, I always had a deeper sense that no matter what I'd face during my time on Earth, it would all make sense in the end.

We may not always understand why we go through hard times or why some of us experience more difficult times than others, but I've found comfort in the belief that there is always a higher purpose for our struggles. This may not make the hard times easier or less painful, but it reminds me that there's more going on than what I can see with my own eyes. There's a bigger picture, and I'm not the only one influencing the outcome. I'm not the one ultimately in control.

Soon after that moment in the car, I had the opportunity to discuss surrender with Kute Blackson, a transformational teacher, visionary, and bestselling author. He was releasing a book called *The Magic of Surrender: Finding the Courage to Let Go*, and I invited him to be a guest on my podcast. Our conversation was fascinating.[39]

Kute told me he defines surrender as openhearted participation with the process of life. "I think of the universe as divine love," he said, "and surrender means opening ourselves to that love and how it's unfolding. The illusion that we control everything actually blocks us from receiving wisdom and opportunities from the universe. To receive those, we must let go of control."

This reminded me that we all have to surrender eventually: if not today or tomorrow, then at the point of death, like my grandfather did. Surrender means you stop forcing life to conform to your plans. In Kute's words, you "let go of this idea of who you *should* be, how things *should* be in your life, the life you *should* be living, how you think your relationships *should* be, so you can open to the life you're really, truly, authentically meant to live."

I couldn't agree more.

Our culture associates the word *surrender* with weakness or giving up. We fear releasing control because we think things won't work out if we do. But that definition of surrender misses the fact that true surrender is actually strength. It takes incredible courage to accept the power and wisdom of forces beyond your control.

I told Kute that as much as I had thought I was letting go throughout my journey, it wasn't until I saw my grandpa surrender that I understood what full surrender looked like. When we surrender, we relax and let the forces beyond us step in and take it from there.

Resistance makes everything harder and more exhausting. If life is taking you one way and you are fighting for it to go another, you won't get very far. It's like swimming upstream in a river: You can do it for a minute, but eventually you'll exhaust yourself trying to force your way through.

Surrender allows you to flow down the path of least resistance, relax into what is, and find an effortless way to live. Instead of swimming upstream, you go along for the ride and see where it takes you. You never know: You may end up somewhere way more beautiful than you ever could have imagined.

This doesn't mean you shouldn't try to solve problems. In some cases, putting up a strong fight is incredibly important—for example, if you're enduring abuse, injustice, or a health condition. The point is to choose your battles. Surrender doesn't mean giving in or giving up; it means trusting the process.

Trust is essential to surrender, but most people get it backward. They think trust means believing everything will work out *their way*. How often have you caught yourself thinking, *I trust it will all work out*, when what you really mean is, *This had better work out like I'd planned*? That's not surrender—that's bargaining with the universe. And it never works.

Surrender doesn't mean giving up or putting in zero effort; it's about fine-tuning *where* you put your effort. Remember, we are in a co-creating relationship with the universe and God. When we surrender, we give our effort where the universe directs us.

On my podcast, Kute explained this with a surfing metaphor. "Sometimes surfers sit on their boards for twenty or thirty minutes just waiting for a wave. They're not out there with a hose trying to *make* a wave. They know they can't control the ocean. Instead, they trust a wave is coming. And once the wave comes, they're all in," he said.

Surrender means participating instead of forcing or resisting. It's about allowing the ocean of life to carry you while making the most of the ride.

How can you tell when you've truly surrendered? For one thing, you'll be less exhausted. Things will start to feel light and effortless instead of heavy and effortful.

Every time I competed in snowboarding, I worked my butt off and gave it everything I had. Even in the start gates, I kept my mind on what I needed to do to win the race until the very moment the gate dropped. Then I let go and handed myself over to the race. I knew I'd put in my work. It was time, as they say, to let go and let God—to trust that the universe would take me the rest of the way.

It's the same with speaking. My talks may look effortless, but that's because I work harder than anyone I know developing and preparing them. I will work on a speech for weeks before I go onstage. But as soon as I hear "Amy Purdy" announced over the big speakers and my walk-on music begins to play, I completely surrender to the moment.

I'm no longer thinking or controlling. I'm just *there*. I trust that I did my part, and now it's time for the universe to do its part.

Do your work, and the universe will rise up to meet you. When you make careful preparations and then let go of the outcome, you make space for magic to happen.

TOOL: SURRENDER CONTROL

One of the most important lessons we can learn in life is knowing when to let go of the fight and lean in to the flow. Sometimes the things we're doing to protect ourselves are actually dragging us down—and when we let go of those defenses, life begins to move in unexpected ways. Here are five ways you can surrender and ride the wave of life:

1. Don't assume.

Don't assume you know the universe's plans for you. Instead, allow it to guide you and embrace the freedom that comes from not knowing all the answers.

I once saw a story about a woman whose doctor said her breast cancer would be the hardest fight of her life. But instead of just fighting, she surrendered to the experience, and it brought her closer to her family, inspired her to travel, and helped her live more fully than ever before.

A friend of mine spent seventeen years pursuing her childhood dream of becoming a philosopher at a prestigious university abroad. When it fell through, she was devastated. But within days of returning to the US, an uncanny series of events led to a new home, amazing friendships, and a career she enjoyed even more than philosophy.

We can't assume we know where we will end up—or how we'll feel about it once we're there. We have to let go, trust in the universe, and allow it to take us in the direction of least resistance.

2. Have faith in your co-creator.

When I was younger, whenever I would get scared of something bad happening, my mom would say, "Amy, at times like these, you just need to have faith." To this day, simply remembering those words is enough to comfort me.

Remind yourself that you're not alone. You are a co-creator with God and the universe. You don't have to exhaust yourself making something happen that isn't happening. Give your best effort, then let the universe carry the rest.

Even if you don't know your spiritual beliefs, just trusting that you aren't the only force in the world controlling your life can give you a sense of peace, comfort, and ease.

3. Trust in the bigger picture.

In order to surrender, you must trust that life is unfolding exactly as it should, even if it's uncomfortable at times. Sometimes we go through something difficult on our way to something extraordinary. Keep your eye on the bigger picture, and trust that whatever hardships you're going through will be meaningful in the end.

4. Consider the worst-case scenario.

What's the worst-case scenario for your situation? If you can accept it, then you're free.

Say you're in a toxic work environment and you want to speak up. What's the worst-case scenario—getting fired? If you can accept that outcome, you're free to go to HR or contact the CEO with your concerns. No matter what happens, you can move forward. Getting fired might even mean you find a much better job.

Want to start a business? If you can accept the worst-case scenario that you might fail, you're free to make better decisions without the fear of failure holding you back. In fact, failure might teach you lessons that will help you build a better business down the road.

At one point, doctors told me that losing my legs and having a kidney transplant was the worst-case scenario for me. After it happened, I ended up with the most incredible, adventurous, blessed life beyond anything I could have imagined!

5. Release attachment.

Attachment to outcomes leads to suffering. Hanging on to the past, beliefs of how you think life should be, or situations that aren't serving you can all cause needless resistance.

Release your attachments to these things. This will help open you to what comes next.

When you get too attached, you start swimming upstream and losing your precious energy. Instead, release what was and accept what is. Remember, your tight grip isn't keeping you safe—it's keeping you stuck.

—

Life is more than what you see before you. There are hidden forces at play: timing, connections, opportunities, and challenges that are shaping your path in ways you may not yet fully understand. Trusting this unseen wisdom allows you to release fear, anxiety, and resistance, making space for clarity, growth, and unexpected blessings.

Give room for life to flow and take you to places you never could have expected. Remember, surrender isn't giving up—it's learning to trust the wave beneath you.

You aren't here to fight the current. You're here to ride it.

NINETEEN

ALONE IN THE UNIVERSE to *Divine Intervention*

I CAN'T TELL YOU HOW MANY TIMES I lay on my couch in 2019, 2020, and 2021 and wondered, *Where are my miracles?*

Two decades ago, when I was fighting for my life, I'd experienced so many miracles. When I entered the hospital in septic shock and full organ failure, the on-site surgeon, Dr. Abby, told my family he had never seen anyone pull out of something like this. "It would be an absolute miracle if she survives the night," he said. "You should gather family to come say their goodbyes."

When I survived and left the hospital, the local news ran a story about me. My primary care doctor told them, "There are some things you can't explain. Divine intervention absolutely played a role in Amy surviving this."

My kidney transplant was another miracle. Every time I tell a doctor I've been living with a donated kidney for twenty-four years with no issues, they say, "You're in the 1 percent. You're a walking miracle." And I feel that way too.

I truly believe that going through hardship brings you nearer to the divine than anything else, especially when it brings you close to death.

When I look back at those tough months in the hospital and the years of recovery that came after, I feel deep gratitude for all the miracles that happened along the way.

But now, having accepted there was nothing more I could do for my leg, I couldn't help but wonder, *Where are all my miracles now?*

Other than the experience I had in the hospital in Boston when my grandfather passed, I hadn't felt any divine intervention on this journey the way I had before. The absence of miracles scared me. I wondered if I'd just been romanticizing those earlier days. I thought, *Did those miracles really happen? And if they happened then, why aren't they happening now? Where are those magical moments I need so badly?*

It had now been twenty-five months since my injury, and I had no idea what the path forward would look like. All I knew was that if I ever wanted to walk comfortably in my prosthetic again, I'd need a miracle—because it was clear there was nothing else we could do.

I knew one thing for certain: I didn't want to live in pain for the rest of my life. I decided that if my leg continued to hurt and the pain prevented me from walking in a prosthetic, I would take the last course of action available to me: amputate my left leg above the knee. This would be a big change from being a below-the-knee amputee. It takes much more energy, high-tech prosthetics, and knee joints to walk. But it would maximize blood flow and therefore minimize or even eliminate pain.

But before proceeding with the amputation, I wanted to see what my body would do on its own. I decided to give it until November of that year. This would give my leg about eight months to do what it was going to do without my surgeons or me intervening.

All along, an above-knee amputation had been what I was fighting so hard to avoid. Now I felt some comfort in having it as an option. Knowing I still had a path that could free me from pain helped calm my mind.

The truth is, I knew I would be okay even if my leg was amputated above the knee. Some of my closest friends were world champion athletes with above-the-knee amputations. Being a Paralympian and running a program for disabled athletes, I knew so many above-the-knee amputees who were absolutely thriving. Although I fought the amputation, I had plenty of examples showing me that even if I lost my leg above the knee, I would be okay. There was still an option to live a full, active, pain-free life.

I spent the next few months relaxing as much as I could. I still spoke for some events, but my talks were mostly virtual. Instead, I focused on self-care, doing everything I could to help my body recover from all it had been through. I ate healthy food, worked out by doing floor exercises, slept, read, and swam. Daniel and I went to Antigua and relaxed on the beach for a week. My leg didn't feel good, but I tried to relax and to enjoy a more normal pace of life. I thought, *What will be will be.*

One morning in June, I woke up, and my leg felt surprisingly good. In fact, it felt the best it had in years. The following day it still felt good, and for an entire week it continued to feel strangely normal.

I called Dr. Mubarak. "My leg feels surprisingly amazing," I said. "Can we do an ultrasound to see what's going on?"

The results shocked us.

When the tech followed my blocked femoral artery down to my knee, we saw something incredible: a glimmer of red. Right next to my blocked femoral artery was a bright-red pipe of blood nearly the same size running right alongside it, from my hip all the way down to my knee!

All this time, we'd been fighting to keep my artery open, but as soon as it shut down, my body took over and created a new one.

When an artery closes, a series of small collateral vessels will sometimes develop to help deliver blood. However, those arteries are usually so small that you can barely see them on an ultrasound.

This collateral artery was different. It wasn't small and twisted but large and straight. It didn't even look like a collateral artery—it looked like my body had created a brand-new femoral artery. It branched into two smaller arteries below my knee, sending blood below the knee when I didn't even have a foot that required it.

If that wasn't a miracle, I didn't know what was.

My doctors and I had zero control over making this happen. And yet it did. It was almost as if when my artery shut down and I threw my hands up in surrender, my body said, "I got this."

After years of surgeries and fighting to save my leg, it eventually saved itself.

For me, this was an important reminder that miracles don't always happen on our timeline. Because of my previous experience fighting for my life, I assumed that divine intervention would come through for me on my hardest of days. When divine help didn't arrive at exactly the moment I expected it to, I started questioning if there was a God. *Where are my angels? Where is that miraculous energy I felt before?*

Now I realized that the divine had been with me all along—it just hadn't been following my schedule.

I do believe I needed all the medical intervention I had. Ultimately, it bought the time my body needed to heal. When the injury happened and the artery first closed in 2019, there were zero collateral arteries, and that's why it was such a dire situation. As my doctors and I worked to preserve my leg and keep blood flowing over the years, we gave it time to sort itself out.

And *yet* had my artery not completely closed itself off in March, it wouldn't have been forced to make this new pathway.

Miracles are the perfect example of how we co-create our reality. In my case, medical intervention was definitely necessary, but when it came time to stop medical intervention, the divine had the space it needed to step in.

Of course, I can choose to explain the miracles in my life in a purely scientific way, especially ones concerning my health. I'm a science-minded gal. I love studying research and learning how everything works. But there are some things that are too perfect to be explained only with science. I choose to see those moments as divine intervention.

Because I've experienced so many miracles, I'm always looking for them. You can choose to look at the world like everything is a miracle, or you can look at the world like nothing is a miracle—it's up to you. I choose to look at the world, our bodies, nature, and the seemingly too-good-to-be-true, "coincidental" moments of my life with complete and utter awe.

This has been key to me living a good life: choosing to see the magic around me and believing there is more going on than what we can see with our own eyes.

I believe there is a creative, spiritual, divine force that flows through each and every one of us. This force connects us, guides us, and reminds us that we are never alone. This belief has carried me through moments of deep loss and challenge and propelled me toward the greatest experiences and accomplishments of my life.

If you look at the world like everything is a miracle, you begin to see miracles everywhere. And you will feel and benefit from the magic they bring to your life.

TOOL: LOOK FOR MIRACLES

We tend to think of miracles as dramatic, once-in-a-lifetime events that defy all explanation. But life is actually full of miracles hidden in plain sight—moments of unexpected connection, divine timing, and simple wonder. Here are my favorite ways to see and experience more miracles:

1. Cultivate awe.

When you look at life with a sense of awe and wonder, you will see miracles everywhere. This isn't putting on rose-tinted glasses; it's putting on *hyperclarity* glasses and opening your eyes to the wonders constantly unfolding around you.

One easy way to nurture your sense of awe is to reflect on the human body. The human body is *amazing.* It's perfectly put together. No matter what shape your body is in, it is perfect, and all the systems that are keeping you alive are perfect. Even when it may not be working at its best, it is resilient. It is built to survive, and every system works in sync with the others to do exactly that.

Another way to cultivate awe is to pay attention to nature. This whole planet and the animals and plants that call it home exist in a symbiotic relationship. Everything feeds everything else in a grand circle of life—even death creates life. That circle of life is a miracle.

Anytime you need to fill your cup of wonder, go outside. Look at the trees. Look at the flowers. Look at the beautiful sunrises and sunsets. Look at the clouds that make the rain that nourishes all of us.

Allow yourself to bathe in the wonder of the world. The more wonder you feel, the more wonder you'll find.

2. Surrender.

Make room for miracles to appear. Lay down control over the things that are out of your hands.

When I was with Oprah for the *Life You Want Tour*, she told a story I'll never forget. She said that after she auditioned for the movie *The Color Purple*, she wanted the role so badly it was all she could think about. She waited for weeks to hear back from the producers and nearly drove herself mad obsessing over the things she could have done differently in her audition.

One day while on a jog, she fell to her knees and cried. She let all the stress she was feeling pour out of her. For the first time, she handed the outcome over to God and the universe. She surrendered purely and utterly. She said she truly laid it down and released all control of the outcome.

The next day, she got a call and was told she got the part.

This story always sticks with me because it's the perfect example of how when we let go of control, we allow miracles to happen.

3. Harness the power of connection.

My friend Rachel Platten, a platinum award-winning singer-songwriter, was dealing with severe back pain around the time of my injury.

She reached out to me one day in desperation. I immediately connected her to Nicole Sachs, a therapist with a podcast called *The Cure for Chronic Pain*. Nicole's therapy treats pain through the mind and emotions, using practices like journaling to release trauma.

Rachel and Nicole started working together, and today Rachel is pain-free. She told me, "Amy, it's a miracle. I couldn't even move! You saved my life."

This miracle only happened thanks to connection—me with Nicole, Rachel with me, then the two of them together. Connection creates miracles.

If you are looking for a miracle, reach out to the people around you. You never know when one of them will hold the key.

4. Believe in miracles.

Choose to believe that there is something bigger than what you can see. Maybe it's God. Maybe it's love. Maybe it's the divine creative energy that flows through all that exists, even the leaves on the trees.

However you choose to account for miracles, start looking for them in your life. Miracles *do* happen every single day—you just have to practice surrendering control and opening your eyes and heart to see them. I know because I am a walking miracle myself.

—

Miracles aren't rare events reserved for a select few people; they're a constant presence in our lives when we take the time to look. When you cultivate awe, surrender control, connect with others, and believe in forces bigger than yourself, you don't just see more miracles. You realize you *are* one.

TWENTY

SELF-DOUBT to *Self-Confidence*

IN THE SUMMER OF 2021, my surgery days were behind me. Since the spontaneous, miraculous growth of the new arterial system, my doctors and I felt confident that my leg would continue to improve over time.

Back in 2019, I'd started this whole ordeal expecting three phases of recovery: saving my leg, healing my leg, and then fitting a new prosthetic. More than two years later, I still hadn't moved onto phase three, but I knew my leg was getting healthier.

The cloud that had been hanging over my life started to lift at the same time as the COVID restrictions. This meant I was receiving invitations to speak in person again. I'd gotten so used to speaking to the tiny lens on my laptop. It had been so long since I'd spoken *live* in front of an audience that the thought of walking onstage felt foreign.

The world had changed during the pandemic—but so had I. The changes weren't just physical. They got to the core of who I believed myself to be. Even though I had just overcome the toughest years of my life, I felt smaller, more vulnerable, and less confident than I had before.

The thought of going onstage again after more than a year of speaking virtually made me nervous. In the past, my speaking gigs had typically been sandwiched between weeks of travel and back-to-back snowboard races. I would show up to talks coming off adrenaline-fueled highs with tons of energy and stories to share. I would strut out in my carbon fiber legs, three-inch heels, and a short dress with my head held high.

By the summer of 2021, I couldn't wear a dress to show my legs because I was still using crutches—and I certainly couldn't wear heels. On top of that, I had to sit on a stool instead of walking back and forth across the stage, which had always been my preference.

But more importantly, I no longer *felt* like the person I once was. In fact, I didn't really know *who* I felt like. Sometimes I'd look back at old photos from before my injury and my heart would sink knowing that strong, confident version of myself didn't exist anymore. Although nothing could take away what I'd accomplished, it felt impossible to embody the person I'd once been.

Hardship can either build a strong outer shell that toughens you up or it can soften you and break you down. I felt I'd gone through the latter. I asked myself, *How am I supposed to walk onstage and talk to thousands of people about how to believe in themselves when I'm feeling so uncertain about myself?*

I found my answer by reflecting on my past. I realized that for all my previous accomplishments, whether it was showing up to my first snowboarding competition, standing onstage for my very first speech, or stepping onto the dance floor for my first dance on *Dancing with the Stars,* I had always been nervous. I'd always been unsure, and I'd never felt ready.

But I did it anyway. And eventually the confidence came.

I realized the same concept applied here: I felt nervous, but I just had to *do it anyway*.

I caught a flight to my talk, crutched onto the stage, sat on a stool, and spoke to the audience about navigating change and uncertainty. I felt vulnerable and awkward at times. But I did it anyway.

I did it because all my past experiences had taught me a crucial secret: Confidence comes later.

Most people want to feel confident *before* they do something new. They take their lack of confidence as a sign that they should stop before they've even gotten started.

They don't realize that confidence never comes before you do something—it builds through the process of doing it.

When I signed up for *Dancing with the Stars*, I had no idea what I was doing. Dancing with prosthetic feet was hard. I would walk onto the dance floor, my feet would slip out from underneath me, and I'd have to use all my core muscles to stabilize myself. The only way to get through was to roll my shoulders back, lift my chin up, put my game face on, and do it anyway, even when I was terrified.

The show was aired live. Right after we performed, the votes would roll in, and so would the Facebook and Instagram comments. Some comments were nice . . . and some were not so nice. But a surprising number of them pertained to my confidence. People would say either, "Wow, I love how confident Amy is!" or "Amy is overconfident."

This fascinated me because the truth was, I wasn't confident at all.

I had never danced before. Every time I stepped onto that dance floor, my heart would pound, my knees would shake, and my vision would blur. I'm sure I even mentally blacked out a few times!

Hearing people comment on my confidence, or even my "overconfidence," was a stark contrast to what I was actually feeling inside.

Looking back, I now see that the thing people perceived as confidence—me walking out with my shoulders back and head held high—was actually me mustering up everything I had to push myself out there.

It wasn't confidence they were seeing. It was courage.

Eventually, after weeks and weeks of practicing and pushing myself to show up every Monday night, I began to trust myself. I began to realize that I wasn't going to die if I made a mistake in my dance. I would survive, and I would actually do better than I expected.

Dancing live on TV week after week developed my *competence*, which then built my *confidence.* I began to trust that I could not only do the dances but also do them while afraid and under pressure. As my competence grew bit by bit, so did my confidence, and I began to trust that even if I didn't feel ready, I would figure it out.

It took a lot of courage to show up every week unsure of myself, but I kept showing up no matter how scared I was. Over time, I built the confidence I needed to make it to the end of the season.

And do you know what's crazy? I almost won the show! Derek and I came in second place. Who would have thought a girl who lost her legs would go on to almost win a dance show?

When companies began inviting me to speak in person in the summer of 2021, I remembered that it wasn't confidence I needed to get back out there but courage. As long as I was courageous, the confidence would come.

And so, speech by speech, I stepped onstage using my crutches and slowly found my voice again. I began showing up not as someone pretending to be the old me but as the person becoming the new me. By practicing courage over and over, I eventually built my confidence back and have since spoken on stages all across the world.

Neuroscience shows that practicing courage activates the prefrontal cortex—the rational, decision-making part of your brain—and helps override the amygdala, the fear center. In other words, courage is like a muscle you can strengthen. When you practice being brave, it gets easier every time. Your brain starts defaulting to *I can do this* instead of *I should run away.*

—

As I was rebuilding my confidence onstage, I also yearned to rebuild it in my body.

I had never imagined that snowboarding would someday cease to be a part of my life. For years, I'd been telling people that snowboarding saved my life after I lost my legs. Snowboarding is how I met my husband. It's how we built our organization. It's what launched my career as a Paralympian and a speaker, and it's where I found my courage and my confidence. It made me the person I am today.

As I sit here and work on this book, it's been six years since I've been able to snowboard. At times, this loss has been heartbreaking. The thing that brought me the most freedom and confidence in my life, I haven't been able to do.

This was one more area of my life where I had to let go of the Old Amy and learn to embrace the New Amy. Instead of trying to go back to who I was before, I had to consider other options. I asked myself, *What CAN I do? What other activities might give me the same quality of experience as snowboarding?*

In chapter 11, I told you about how I used my value diagram to figure out that surfing might be a great way to help me feel physically strong, capable, and confident again.

In the summer of 2022, Daniel and I booked a trip to Maui.

This wasn't my first time surfing. I had tried it a few years before my injury and loved it. At the time, however, I was using my legs, so it felt a lot like snowboarding. This time, I wouldn't be able to do that. Surfing without my legs was completely out of my comfort zone. Would it even be possible? And if it was possible, would I enjoy it?

Up until that point, I'd never done any kind of sport without my legs. I had also become physically weak after not walking for years. I'd lost an enormous amount of muscle. I worried the waves might just throw me around. Also, real talk—I'm terrified of sharks. I've already lost enough body parts for one lifetime, and I'm not trying to lose more!

But I knew pushing myself physically and mentally was important, and if I could find a love for surfing like I had for snowboarding, it would be worth it.

In the words of Brené Brown, "We can choose courage or we can choose comfort but we can't have both."

I chose courage.

Daniel and I invited a group of our Adaptive Action Sports athletes to Maui with us to test the waters. There's no better way to learn to do something new than to gather a group of friends who are in the same boat as you! We went out with our surf coach, and I absolutely fell in love with surfing.

The fact that I was out of my comfort zone lit me up inside. The element of fear and uncertainty gave me a feeling of excitement I hadn't experienced in a long time. I got butterflies in my stomach, and blood pumped hard through my body as I headed out into the waves. I loved feeling my body work again as I paddled out and got up on my knees on the board.

After a few days of surfing, I felt stronger and more confident than I had in years. Was I a pro? No, but I was doing something new, and I felt alive again!

At one point I paddled out into a wave that turned out to be bigger than I'd expected. Instead of avoiding it, I paddled as hard as I could, got up on my knees, and hit it just right. I leaned onto the rail and into the wave. The feeling reminded me of what it was like to ride my snowboard on a fresh powder day: like riding on a cloud. To me, this was the most effortless and satisfying feeling in the world—and now I'd just found it again in surfing.

I left Maui feeling more capable, confident, and stronger than I had in years. I felt so grateful I'd had the courage to try.

Some people think courage is an innate trait you either have or don't. But the truth is that courage is a choice and a practice. Every time you choose to try something new or put yourself out there, you are practicing courage.

After spending most of my adult life around Olympic and Paralympic athletes, motivational speakers, and some of the most well-known entrepreneurs and public figures in the world, I can tell you without a doubt that the most successful people aren't the ones born with confidence—they're the ones who practice courage. They're the ones putting themselves out there, willing to try new things, willing to fail over and over, and willing to start again until they eventually figure it out.

My friend, business and marketing coach Amy Porterfield, says in her bestselling book, *Two Weeks Notice*, "Courage is something you choose. Confidence is something you earn."

Don't wait to build up your confidence before putting yourself out there and trying new things. Practice the courage to go for it anyway, *before you feel ready.*

Confidence comes in the doing. When you choose to do the things that scare you the most, you realize just how capable you really are.

TOOL: BUILD CONFIDENCE THROUGH COURAGE

Confidence grows through repeated acts of courage. The more challenges you face, the more you learn to trust yourself to handle them. Each time you push through fear and uncertainty, you're stacking up evidence that you're more capable than you realized. Here are five ways to turn courage into confidence:

1. Normalize discomfort.

Discomfort is a normal part of the process of stretching yourself and trying new things. It's okay to be uncomfortable; in fact, it's a sign of growth. The more you welcome discomfort, the easier it becomes, the more familiar it feels, and the less intimidating it is.

I love this quote by boxer Ed Latimore: "Embarrassment is the cost of entry. If you aren't a foolish beginner, you will never be a graceful master."

Remember this when you're putting yourself out there. Every graceful master was once a foolish beginner. Discomfort is the price we pay to explore and improve our abilities. Think of it as an investment in yourself: Pay the price of discomfort now to benefit from competence and confidence later.

2. Take small risks daily.

Courage isn't about eliminating fear but about acting in spite of it. Start with small challenges that push you outside your comfort zone, whether it's speaking up in a meeting, trying a new activity, or sharing a story online. Every small act of bravery compounds over time.

Taking small risks is like flexing a courage muscle. The more often you flex it, the stronger it becomes across all areas of your life.

3. Reframe fear as growth.

Feeling nervous or scared isn't a sign that you're incapable—it just means that you care.

Rather than seeing fear as a stop sign, see it as a signal that you're expanding your limits. This mindset shift makes fear feel like an invitation instead of a barrier: You're becoming the person you want to be.

When you feel afraid, ask yourself, *What's the best thing that could happen?* and *How will I grow from this?*

Write your answers down and revisit them often.

4. Stack small wins.

Every time you take a courageous step, acknowledge it. Confidence grows when you recognize your progress.

Celebrate the steps you've taken, even if you felt afraid, uncomfortable, or like you "failed" in some way. Ask yourself, *What have I learned? How have I grown?*

When you see how far you've come, you'll begin to trust yourself more. When you acknowledge your wins, you're building a body of evidence that you can do hard things.

5. Expand your comfort zone slowly.

My snowboarding coach used to say, "Confidence builds confidence." In other words, don't tackle something so huge that it paralyzes you. Instead, start by stepping slightly out of your comfort zone. Once you gain confidence in small steps, you can push yourself further and further outside your old limits.

I once heard from a girl whose illness had left her with scars all over her body. She lived in Florida and used to love lying on the beach in her swimsuit but felt so insecure about being stared at that she thought she might never feel confident on the beach again. She'd recently gone to the beach completely covered from head to toe, yearning to feel free in her swimsuit again.

I knew from experience that people look when they're curious. People have been staring at me and my legs for years, and that wasn't going to change. I encouraged her to build her tolerance for being looked at.

"The more you cover up," I said, "the more insecure you're going to feel." I suggested she start by wearing shorts to the beach to expose her scars just a little bit.

"After you get comfortable wearing shorts," I continued, "try wearing a bikini top with your shorts, even if it's just for a few minutes.

The point was to expand her comfort zone gradually.

She started exposing her scars. Little by little, she began to build confidence and trust that she'd be okay.

Courage doesn't always require a huge leap; it's mostly a series of small steps that expand your comfort zone over time.

—

The more you practice courage, the more courageous you will become—and the more confident you will feel. Each brave choice rewires your brain to see challenges as opportunities rather than as threats. What looks like a terrifying leap today will feel like no big deal tomorrow. Once you take the first step, you may be surprised by just how far you go.

TWENTY-ONE

SETBACK to *Comeback*

SOON AFTER MY BODY DECIDED to grow that beautiful, miraculous collateral artery in 2021, my team and I began the process of making a new prosthetic leg for me to walk in.

Prosthetics are the opposite of one size fits all; you can't just breeze into a prosthetics shop and stroll out with a new leg the way you could with a new pair of shoes. Each one is custom-made and requires many iterations to get exactly right. Every millimeter determines whether a leg supports you, feels too tight, or digs in. The tiniest change can either destroy a prosthetic's fit or make it just right. This is why my injury was such a big deal—it meant I had to abandon the prosthetic that had served me for decades of my life and start this arduous process over from scratch.

I knew that getting a prosthetic leg to fit right again would take a long time, but I had no idea just how much patience it would require. I spent hundreds of hours in the prosthetic shop with my team. We made legs that fit almost perfectly, only to accidentally destroy them. We made legs that fit great one day, only to have my leg cramp severely every time I put them on. We made legs that stopped fitting after two weeks, suddenly too tight or lacking support. We started over so many times that I lost count.

What made the journey particularly grueling was my leg's uniqueness. The experimental surgeries in Boston had saved my leg by shortening it and reconstructing the muscles. But I ended up in an unusual situation: I had more muscle engagement than ever before, which is great for blood flow but not great for wearing a prosthetic leg made of rigid carbon fiber.

As high tech as prosthetics are, they can also be quite barbaric. Our bodies are made of soft tissue that needs to move and flex, and yet in a prosthetic, they're confined inside rock-solid carbon fiber that doesn't flex or expand at all. Now that my leg muscles wanted to grow and expand, getting a prosthetic to fit had become incredibly challenging. Throughout my life, I've made walking, snowboarding, and dancing in prosthetics look easy—and for a while, it was. But this experience was a reminder of how difficult it can be.

The crazy part was, my leg was healthier now than I ever imagined it would be. All I wanted to do was put my leg on and go! I wanted to run. I wanted to hike. I wanted to get on my snowboard again, but I couldn't. At least, not *yet*.

Each prosthetic we made brought me a little closer. At one point, I couldn't walk from my bedroom to my kitchen island without my leg cramping. Then I made it to my front door. Then to my mailbox.

The mailbox moment was huge for me. When I first injured my leg back in 2019, that hotshot surgeon told me I may not be able to walk to my mailbox again—ever. At the time, I feared it would take six months to prove him wrong. It ended up taking close to six years, but eventually I did walk to my mailbox. Then I even walked past my mailbox to the end of my driveway. (To give myself even more credit, my driveway is really long!)

The moment I walked past the mailbox and halfway up our beautiful mountain street brought me to tears. After years of not giving up on myself despite all the negative voices (sometimes my own) telling me I'd never do it, I had proven that as long as you keep going, you will eventually make it to the other side.

I hadn't bounced *back* to who I once was. Instead, with time, growth, and patience, I had bounced *forward* into a new me: a wiser, calmer, more present version of myself. And what made this possible was perseverance.

—

Here's what I learned about perseverance over those months and years of fighting to walk again: It's not about never wanting to quit. It's about choosing to keep showing up, no matter how hard things get. It's driving to one more appointment when you want to give up hope. It's trying *one more tiny adjustment* when you've already tried ten thousand. It's refusing to give in to despair and insisting that your solution is out there somewhere—you just have to keep looking.

Sometimes perseverance can look like stubbornness or even denial. When other people doubt that your goal is achievable, it's easy to start doubting yourself: *Come on, Amy. Why can't you just accept that this is as good as it gets?* But everybody who ever achieved a difficult goal was told it couldn't be done. Whereas denial comes from a rigid and fearful insistence on having things go your way, perseverance is powered by courage, adaptability, and a strong sense of purpose.

As of this book's publication, I still haven't arrived at the perfect prosthetic that lets me do all the activities I used to love, although I'm getting closer every day. My team and I are still iterating, still going back to the drawing board over and over again. Are there days when I want to cry in frustration? Plenty—but I know that quitting won't get me where I want to be. Only persevering will.

Of course, this doesn't mean that quitting is *never* the right answer or that every battle is worth fighting until the bitter end. Only you know what you're willing to endure and for how long. Only you know how much you're willing to sacrifice. Only you know how much pushing is within healthy limits and how much will drive you crazy, drain your spirit, or take too much time away from other things. These decisions can't be up to someone else.

You choose your battles. *You* determine whether you want to keep pressing forward or step back and accept where you are today. Everyone's journey is different. One person who has cancer may choose to fight to the very end while another person may decide to relax and enjoy the time they have left. There is no right or wrong. Whatever your heart tells you is what's right for you.

Perseverance isn't a one-size-fits-all solution; it's appropriate in some situations and inappropriate in others, and you're the only one who can make that call. If you're feeling drained and depleted by the battle, and the resources you've allocated to it are taking away from other things you value in life, it's okay to change gears. Sometimes strength means accepting the things you can't change.

Nobody navigates this question more gracefully than the disabled community. For far too long, people with disabilities have been made to feel that there is something wrong with them or that their bodies are broken and need fixing. On social media, you see viral videos of people standing up from their wheelchairs and walking again, with thousands of comments like "Congrats for not giving up!" or "If you want it bad enough, you will achieve it!"

As inspiring as these videos can be, the underlying message—that if you work hard enough, you can beat your disability—simply isn't everyone's reality. And it shouldn't have to be.

Many people, like me, wholeheartedly embrace their disability as an important part of who they are. People with disabilities don't need to be fixed. What needs to be fixed are the limitations the world places on people with disabilities. In many cases, the disability itself isn't the problem—it's the lack of accessibility.

These days, people with disabilities are rising up to share a message of acceptance. It means no longer saying, "I'm bound to a wheelchair," but instead, "I use a wheelchair." It means saying, "Yes, I can't walk. But I don't *need* to walk." It's a movement that declares, "I am whole just as I am."

I love this perspective because it reflects how I've always felt about having two prosthetic legs. When people tell me, "I'm so sorry you lost your legs," I respond, "Are you kidding? This has been the greatest gift of my life. Look where these carbon fiber legs have taken me!"

My friend Alana Nichols exemplifies this beautifully. She was paralyzed in a snowboarding accident and now uses a wheelchair. She has won a wall of Paralympic medals competing in basketball and alpine skiing, travels the world with her husband and young son using her wheelchair, and even surfs, getting barreled in waves. She lives her best life not in spite of her disability but because of it.

You can absolutely thrive when you embrace where you are.

The key for me has always been accepting my situation and asking, *Where do I want to go from here?* This is how I have always lived: not trying to turn back time but working with what I have right now.

For twenty years, I accepted the loss of my legs, embracing my circumstances without looking back. But since injuring my leg in 2019, I haven't been willing to let go of my mobility. I've chosen to persevere toward my goal in spite of how frustrating and emotionally exhausting it can sometimes be.

Some people say, "Amy, you don't have to walk again to be whole," and I agree. I already felt plenty whole not walking. I'm perfectly whole using my scooter. But I know that I have more steps ahead, and I want to see how far I can go. This has been a consistent theme throughout my life: not trying to go back to what I once was but to continue putting one foot in front of the other and seeing where the path takes me.

As of fall 2025, I'm pain-free and walking up and down the stairs of my three-story house, and it feels so good. I'm walking down the street and onto stages on my own two feet. I'm riding my bike through the trees again and working out in the gym (though very lightly compared to the intense workouts I used to do). I still have a long way to go to get to where I want to be. I'm still on the journey of making a leg that fits well enough to get back to my former activity level, and I still use my scooter for airports and long distances. The fight to walk comfortably and snowboard like I once did continues. Yet at the same time, I accept that I may not be able to achieve what I once did, and I'm okay with that. I accept where I am, yet I still have enough energy in me to see how far I can go.

Perseverance doesn't mean pushing through pain and exhaustion with no relief; it's about pacing yourself. It means listening to your body and spirit and knowing when it's time to rest and when it's time to press forward. After all, the point isn't to crawl over the finish line so broken and depleted that you can't enjoy your achievement. When you reach that goal, you want to have the emotional and physical reserves you need to fully embrace it. Real perseverance honors your humanity, not just your ambition, and it means taking care of yourself throughout your journey.

TOOL: PUT ONE FOOT IN FRONT OF THE OTHER

Whether you're navigating a personal crisis, chasing a long-term goal, or just trying to get through the day, the secret is to choose your battles—and once you've chosen them, commit wholeheartedly and persevere. Here are my favorite ways to keep going in the middle of a climb:

1. Find your support system.

You won't make it far if you rely only on yourself, no matter how strong you are. Surround yourself with people who lift you up, encourage you, and help you regain your strength after you break down and cry.

It takes a team to achieve your goals. Find those who align with you and who can be strong where you are weak.

2. Rest and care for yourself.

Although your problem might feel urgent, you'll burn out if you work without stopping. Instead, take breaks to replenish your energy. Sleep. Eat well. Fill your cup so that you can keep going. When you honor your need for recovery, you come back stronger than before.

3. Keep moving, even if it's slow.

Every step forward is a step forward, and that's all that matters. A goal may take two hours, two weeks, two years, or two decades to achieve. As long as you keep moving toward it, you are getting closer. The only way to fail is to stop moving forward at all.

4. Celebrate the tiny wins.

Don't get discouraged by how far you still have to go. Celebrating tiny wins gives you the resilience you need to keep going. Recognize how far you've already come. Enjoy where you are and remember that you got there only by continuing forward on your journey.

5. Embrace the journey and surrender the outcome. Embracing the journey doesn't mean you enjoy every moment of it. It means you have accepted that it will bring you to your knees at times and that you will need to dig deep to continue.

When you embrace the journey, you embrace what comes your way instead of fighting it. You reserve your energy to use on things you can change and control while accepting the things you can't.

Allow the outcome of your effort to be what it will be. I guarantee that once you reach your goal, you'll look back and realize the journey itself was where the memories and magic were all along.

—

Life's challenges, both the ones we choose and the ones that choose us, aren't obstacles to overcome but opportunities to evolve. Once you accept this truth, life becomes infinitely easier. As long as you're still breathing, you have a life to live, so find meaning in your adversities, persevere through your challenges, keep putting one foot in front of the other, and see how far you can go. You never know—you may end up in a place more beautiful and meaningful than you ever could have imagined.

EPILOGUE

YOU MAY HAVE NOTICED that this book doesn't end with me standing on a mountaintop, triumphantly yelling, "I did it! I overcame all my obstacles and so can you!"

That's because this journey—like life—continues on. I've stood on many mountaintops in victory, and I've also stood in some pretty deep holes, but that's the adventure of life: It keeps coming, surprising you again and again as the years go on.

I intentionally wrote this book knowing I wasn't at the end of my journey but smack dab in the middle of the climb. After all, that's where most of us tend to be.

The injury I endured taught me that the only way to move forward in life is to take one step at a time, even when those steps feel incredibly small. The long recovery and all the ups and downs also gave me time to pay attention to the things that were helping me along the way. This injury forced me to slow down, to be mindful, to celebrate the little wins, and to be grateful for all the blessings in my life, even in the face of adversity.

These days, I continue to give anywhere from thirty to fifty in-person speeches a year—only now, I speak with even deeper conviction, greater purpose, and more heartfelt emotion than before. The depth of what I experienced has helped me connect with myself and with my audiences in a whole new way.

Since my injury, I've traveled all over the world (on my cute scooter, of course). I've spoken on some of the most prestigious stages in the world, appeared on magazine covers, and shared my stories of resilience with a much broader audience. I've grown my business significantly; in fact, at one point I joked, "The more adversity I deal with, the more successful I become!" I was laughing, but it's true: The more obstacles I've had to face, the more valuable my lessons have become.

Throughout all of this, I've fallen more deeply in love with my husband, Daniel, and experienced unconditional love and acceptance from him. We've shared once-in-a-lifetime adventures, like attending the 2024 Summer Olympic Games in Paris, where our room was directly across from the sparkling Eiffel Tower. We've surfed under Hawaiian rainbows, met amazing people, and savored the best food the world has to offer. I even returned to those glamorous Hollywood events—not as the Amy I used to be but as the Amy I am today.

I share this because, as challenging as this journey has been at times, it has been amazing too. Whether it's hard or easy, life is *always* worth fighting for.

If there's one lesson I hope you take from this book, it's that life doesn't end when challenges arise. In fact, challenges are what make life worth living. The hardships we face transform us into better, wiser, fuller versions of ourselves, even if it doesn't feel that way while we're facing them. Life is always going to throw us curveballs, but it's up to us to decide whether we're going to let them break us down or build us into better versions of ourselves.

I gave this book the title *Bounce Forward* instead of *Bounce Back* because every obstacle we face gives us a new tool or perspective that we can use to move forward to something new. The truth is, life isn't about reaching the summit; it's about who we become on the climb. The setbacks, the detours, the moments you wonder if you can even continue—that's where you become the strongest, most resilient version of yourself.

Facing adversity forces you to dig deep and figure out what you're really made of. Each step, even the shaky ones, shapes you into someone stronger, wiser, and more attuned to your own power. After taking my own journey from the deepest valleys to the highest peaks, what I know for sure is this: The most breathtaking views always come after the hardest climbs.

Keep climbing.

FINAL THOUGHTS

BOUNCE FORWARD AND PAY IT FORWARD

Passion is what you do for yourself;
purpose is what you do for others.
—Jim Kwik

I FIRMLY BELIEVE that every breakdown carries the seed of a breakthrough. I don't know if I'll ever snowboard or dance the way I did before. But I know this: Every challenge I've faced has been an opportunity in disguise, an invitation not just to create my best life but to contribute to the world in a new way.

While I was writing this book, a friend of mine became immobile after brain surgery. Insurance wouldn't cover the scooter he needed, so I lent him one I wasn't using. That small gesture filled me with purpose.

Then a mother of three reached out after surviving the same illness I had at nineteen. She'd lost her arms and legs, and insurance wouldn't cover the wheelchair she needed to move around her kitchen and cook for her family.

These moments awakened something in me. I realized I wanted to help others, not just with sports but with the gift of mobility.

Since founding Adaptive Action Sports in 2005, Daniel and I have watched people achieve their dreams, many competing in the Paralympic Games. But we've also seen the heartbreaking reality: Not everyone can afford the specialized equipment, travel, or support they need to participate. Insurance companies consider most mobility equipment a luxury, not a necessity. Meanwhile, a single prosthetic leg can cost anywhere from $20,000 to $80,000. Mind-blowing, right?

Let me be clear: Prosthetic legs and adaptive equipment aren't luxuries. They're the difference between isolation and participation, surviving and thriving, and freedom and confinement. The equipment insurance denies is what allows us to be independent, active, healthy, and, most importantly, contribute to society in a positive way.

Over 1.3 billion people worldwide live with a disability. The longer you live, the more likely you are to join that community. Disability is part of being human. When we recognize that, we start building a world that works for all of us—not just *some* of us.

That's why my husband and I, along with our organization, decided to create the Amy Purdy Fund. This fund alleviates the financial strain associated with physical disabilities by providing financial assistance for mobility equipment and sports-related expenses, whether it's a specialized snowboard prosthetic or a scooter.

Movement has been the greatest gift of my life, and the equipment I rely on—from my carbon fiber legs to my swift little scooter—is what lets me move forward *and* pay it forward.

If I hadn't gone through this injury, I never would have *truly* understood how vital mobility is for a flourishing life—and I never would have created this fund. There is always an opportunity inside the challenge if you choose to look for it.

My passion for snowboarding saved my life, but helping others has given it meaning. I didn't feel truly fulfilled until I began finding ways to turn my struggle into service. Every time someone tells me that hearing about my journey gave them hope or lifted them up in some way, I feel grateful for everything that I've gone through. With the Amy Purdy Fund, I hope to help others in an even more tangible way.

We all are needed in this world, no matter how big or small our contributions are. You don't have to do big public things to make an impact. Your contribution can be your art, your business, your mentorship, or your kindness—anything that connects you to something bigger than yourself. As Steven Pressfield writes in *The War of Art*,[1] "Don't cheat us of your contribution. Give us what you've got."

This is how you create purpose and meaning—not just by bouncing forward but by paying it forward. What feels like pain today is the wisdom you can share tomorrow, and the hardships you've experienced are never wasted when they become someone else's light.

Your journey doesn't end have to end here.
Download the Bounce Forward Tool Kit,
unlock bonus content, and learn more
about the AP Fund by scanning the QR code below!

NOTES

CHAPTER 2: HELPLESS TO *EMPOWERED*

1 Jessica A. Jonikas et al., "Improving Propensity for Patient Self-Advocacy Through Wellness Recovery Action Planning: Results of a Randomized Controlled Trial," *Community Mental Health Journal* 49, no. 3 (2013): 260–69, https://doi.org/10.1007/s10597-011-9475-9.

2 "Fidelity Study Shows Young Professionals on the Move: Six-in-Ten Have Changed Jobs During the Pandemic or Expect to Be at a Different Company Within Two Years," Fidelity Newsroom, 2022, https://newsroom.fidelity.com/pressreleases/fidelity-study-shows-young-professionals-on-the-move—six-in-ten-have-changed-jobs-during-the-pandem/s/30fcad9c-a822-4b51-8f1a-1a61915a6b2e.

CHAPTER 3: ANXIOUS TO *CALM*

3 Lilibet Foster, *Be Here Now: The Andy Whitfield Story*, Silver Lining Entertainment, 2015.

CHAPTER 4: OVERWHELMED TO *COMPOSED*

4 Rich Diviney, *Masters of Uncertainty: The Navy SEAL Way to Turn Stress into Success for You and Your Team* (Amplify, 2025).

CHAPTER 5: WEAK AND ALONE TO *SUPPORTED AND STRONG*

5 Amy Purdy, "Living Beyond Limits," TED Talk, Orange Coast College, CA, May 2011, 9 min., 35 sec., www.ted.com/talks/amy_purdy_living_beyond_limits.

6 Brené Brown, *Daring Greatly: How the Courage to Be Vulnerable Transforms the Way We Live, Love, Parent, and Lead* (Avery, 2012), 34.

7 Marek Jankowski et al., "The Role of Oxytocin in Cardiovascular Protection," *Frontiers in Psychology* 11 (August 2020): 2139, https://doi.org/10.3389/fpsyg.2020.02139.

8 Vivek Jain et al., "Benefits of Oxytocin Administration in Obstructive Sleep Apnea," *American Journal of Physiology–Lung Cellular and Molecular Physiology* 313, no. 5 (November 2017): L825–33, https://doi.org/10.1152/ajplung.00206.2017.

9 Beate Ditzen et al., "Intranasal Oxytocin Increases Positive Communication and Reduces Cortisol Levels During Couple Conflict," *Biological Psychiatry* 65, no. 9 (May 2009): 728–31, https://doi.org/10.1016/j.biopsych.2008.10.011.

CHAPTER 6: FEARING THE UNKNOWN TO *BELIEVING IN THE POSSIBILITIES*

10 Carol Dweck, *Mindset: The New Psychology of Success* (Ballantine Books, 2016), 7.

CHAPTER 8: SELF-CRITICISM TO *SELF-LOVE*

11 Amy Purdy, host, *Bouncing Forward*, podcast, season 1, episode 9, "Liz Gilbert on Getting Through the Most Difficult Moments of Life," March 1, 2021, https://podcasts.apple.com/us/podcast/bouncing-forward-with-amy-purdy/id1546895069?i=1000511128119.

12 Christina Ewert et al., "Self-Compassion and Coping: A Meta-Analysis," *Mindfulness* 12, no. 5 (May 2021): 1063–77, https://doi.org/10.1007/s12671-020-01563-8.

13 Shauna L. Shapiro et al., "Mechanisms of Mindfulness," *Journal of Clinical Psychology* 62, no. 3 (2006): 373–86, https://doi.org/10.1002/jclp.20237.

14 Miguel Bellosta-Batalla et al., "Increased Salivary IgA Response as an Indicator of Immunocompetence After a Mindfulness and Self-Compassion-Based Intervention," *Mindfulness* 9, no. 3 (June 2018): 905–13, https://doi.org/10.1007/s12671-017-0830-y.

CHAPTER 9: NEGATIVE AND NARROW-MINDED TO *OPEN TO NEW PERSPECTIVES*

15 Amy Purdy, host, *Bouncing Forward*, podcast, season 1, episode 21, "Hassan Khan: 5 Characteristics of a Resilient Person," April 12, 2021, https://podcasts.apple.com/us/podcast/bouncing-forward-with-amy-purdy/id1546895069?i=1000516793601.

CHAPTER 10: LOSS AND LACK TO *LIVING ABUNDANTLY*

16 Jo A. Iodice et al., "The Association Between Gratitude and Depression: A Meta-Analysis," *International Journal of Depression and Anxiety* 4, no. 1 (June 2021): 024, https://doi.org/10.23937/2643-4059/1710024.

17 Geyze Diniz et al., "The Effects of Gratitude Interventions: A Systematic Review and Meta-Analysis," *Einstein (São Paulo)* 21 (July 2023): eRW0371, https://doi.org/10.31744/einstein_journal/2023RW0371.

18 Marta Jackowska et al., "The Impact of a Brief Gratitude Intervention on Subjective Well-Being, Biology and Sleep," *Journal of Health Psychology* 21, no. 10 (October 2016): 2207–17, https://doi.org/10.1177/1359105315572455.

19 Laura S. Redwine et al., "Pilot Randomized Study of a Gratitude Journaling Intervention on Heart Rate Variability and Inflammatory Biomarkers in Patients with Stage B Heart Failure," *Psychosomatic Medicine* 78, no. 6 (2016): 667–76, https://doi.org/10.1097/PSY.0000000000000316.

20 Yidi Mao et al., "How Gratitude Inhibits Envy: From the Perspective of Positive Psychology," *PsyCh Journal* 10, no. 3 (June 2021): 384–92, https://doi.org/10.1002/pchj.413.

21 Robert Emmons, "10 Ways to Become More Grateful," *Greater Good Magazine*, November 17, 2010, https://greatergood.berkeley.edu/article/item/ten_ways_to_become_more_grateful1.

CHAPTER 12: STUCK AND STAGNANT TO *CREATING MOMENTUM*

22 Amy Cuddy, "Your Body Language May Shape Who You Are," TED Talk, October 2012, 20 min., 45 sec., www.ted.com/talks/amy_cuddy_your_body_language_may_shape_who_you_are.

23 Amy Purdy, host, *Bouncing Forward*, podcast, season 2, episode 10, "Amy Cuddy: Living Inspired Through Uninspiring Times and the Importance of Supporting One Another," December 20, 2021, https://podcasts.apple.com/us/podcast/bouncing-forward-with-amy-purdy/id1546895069?i=1000545527911.

CHAPTER 13: UNINSPIRED TO *INSPIRED*

24 Amy Purdy, host, *Bouncing Forward*, podcast, season 2, episode 10, "Amy Cuddy: Living Inspired Through Uninspiring Times and the Importance of Supporting One Another," December 20, 2021, https://podcasts.apple.com/us/podcast/bouncing-forward-with-amy-purdy/id1546895069?i=1000545527911.

25 Amy Purdy, host, *Bouncing Forward*, podcast, season 2, episode 3, "Susie Moore: How to Manage Stress and Let It Be Easy to Live a More Inspired Life," November 15, 2021, https://podcasts.apple.com/us/podcast/bouncing-forward-with-amy-purdy/id1546895069?i=1000541977815.

CHAPTER 14: LIMITED TO *LIMITLESS*

26 Maxwell Maltz, *Psycho-Cybernetics: Updated and Expanded* (Tarcher, 2015).

27 Chris P. Neck and Charles C. Manz, "Thought Self-Leadership: The Influence of Self-Talk and Mental Imagery on Performance," *Journal of Organizational Behavior* 13, no. 7 (1992): 681–99, https://doi.org/10.1002/job.4030130705.

28 Peter R. Giacobbi et al., "A Scoping Review of Health Outcomes Examined in Randomized Controlled Trials Using Guided Imagery," *Progress in Preventive Medicine* 2, no. 7 (December 2017): e0010, https://doi.org/10.1097/pp9.0000000000000010.

29 Gail Elliott Patricolo et al., "Beneficial Effects of Guided Imagery or Clinical Massage on the Status of Patients in a Progressive Care Unit," *Critical Care Nurse* 37, no. 1 (February 2017): 62–69, https://doi.org/10.4037/ccn2017282.

30 Marc J. Weigensberg et al., "Effects of Group-Delivered Stress-Reduction Guided Imagery on Salivary Cortisol, Salivary Amylase, and Stress Mood in Urban, Predominantly Latino Adolescents," *Global Advances in Health and Medicine* 11 (February 2022): 21649561211067443, https://doi.org/10.1177/21649561211067443.

31 Maamer Slimani et al., "Effects of Mental Imagery on Muscular Strength in Healthy and Patient Participants: A Systematic Review," *Journal of Sports Science & Medicine* 15, no. 3 (August 2016): 434–50, www.ncbi.nlm.nih.gov/pmc/articles/PMC4974856.

CHAPTER 15: DREAMING TO *CO-CREATING*

32 Christine A. Godwin et al., "Functional Connectivity Within and Between Intrinsic Brain Networks Correlates with Trait Mind Wandering," *Neuropsychologia* 103 (August 2017): 140–53, https://doi.org/10.1016/j.neuropsychologia.2017.07.006.

33 Mel Robbins, host, *The Mel Robbins Podcast*, podcast, episode 227, "#1 Neurosurgeon: How to Manifest Anything You Want & Unlock the Unlimited Power of Your Mind," October 24, 2024, www.melrobbins.com/podcasts/episode-227.

CHAPTER 16: DISCOURAGED TO *HAPPY*

34 Dave Asprey, host, *The Human Upgrade*, podcast, episode 686, "Overcoming Massive Adversity with Little Mind Hacks–Amy Purdy," April 9, 2020, https://daveasprey.com/amy-purdy-686.

35 William Li, *Eat to Beat Disease: The New Science of How Your Body Can Heal Itself* (Grand Central, 2019).

36 Marie Forleo, *Everything Is Figureoutable* (Portfolio, 2019).

CHAPTER 17: GIVING UP TO *FINDING YOUR WAY*

37 Deborah Perkins-Gough, "The Significance of Grit: A Conversation with Angela Lee Duckworth," Association for Supervision and Curriculum Development, September 1, 2013, www.ascd.org/el/articles/the-significance-of-grit-a-conversation-with-angela-lee-duckworth.

38 Angela L. Duckworth et al., "Grit: Perseverance and Passion for Long-Term Goals," *Journal of Personality and Social Psychology* 92, no. 6 (2007): 1087–1101, https://doi.org/10.1037/0022-3514.92.6.1087.

CHAPTER 18: RESISTANCE TO *ACCEPTANCE*

39 Amy Purdy, host, *Bouncing Forward*, podcast, season 1, episode 31, "Kute Blackson: The Magic of Surrender: Why We Need to Let Go of Control and Let Life Flow," May 25, 2021, https://podcasts.apple.com/us/podcast/31-kute-blackson-the-magic-of-surrender-why-we-need/id1546895069?i=1000522911854.

BIBLIOGRAPHY

Asprey, Dave, host. *The Human Upgrade.* Podcast. Episode 686. "Overcoming Massive Adversity with Little Mind Hacks—Amy Purdy." April 9, 2020. https://daveasprey.com/amy-purdy-686.

Bellosta-Batalla, Miguel, Nicolás Ruiz-Robledillo, Patricia Sariñana-González, et al. "Increased Salivary IgA Response as an Indicator of Immunocompetence After a Mindfulness and Self-Compassion-Based Intervention." *Mindfulness* 9, no. 3 (June 2018): 905–13. https://doi.org/10.1007/s12671-017-0830-y.

Brown, Brené. *Daring Greatly: How the Courage to Be Vulnerable Transforms the Way We Live, Love, Parent, and Lead.* Avery, 2012.

Business Wire. "Fidelity Study Shows Young Professionals on the Move: Six-in-Ten Have Changed Jobs During the Pandemic or Expect to Be at a Different Company Within Two Years." Fidelity Newsroom, 2022. https://newsroom.fidelity.com/pressreleases/fidelity-study-shows-young-professionals-on-the-move--six-in-ten-have-changed-jobs-during-the-pandem/s/30fcad9c-a822-4b51-8f1a-1a61915a6b2e.

Cuddy, Amy. "Your Body Language May Shape Who You Are." TED Talk, October 2012. 20 min., 45 sec. www.ted.com/talks/amy_cuddy_your_body_language_may_shape_who_you_are.

Diniz, Geyze, Ligia Korkes, Luca Schiliró Tristão, Rosangela Pelegrini, Patrícia Lacerda Bellodi, and Wanderley Marques Bernardo. "The Effects of Gratitude Interventions: A Systematic Review and Meta-Analysis." *Einstein (São Paulo)* 21 (July 2023): eRW0371. https://doi.org/10.31744/einstein_journal/2023RW0371.

Ditzen, Beate, Marcel Schaer, Barbara Gabriel, Guy Bodenmann, Ulrike Ehlert, and Markus Heinrichs. "Intranasal Oxytocin Increases Positive Communication and Reduces Cortisol Levels During Couple Conflict." *Biological Psychiatry* 65, no. 9 (May 2009): 728–31. https://doi.org/10.1016/j.biopsych.2008.10.011.

Diviney, Rich. *Masters of Uncertainty: The Navy SEAL Way to Turn Stress into Success for You and Your Team.* Amplify, 2025.

Duckworth, Angela L., Christopher Peterson, Michael D. Matthews, and Dennis R. Kelly. "Grit: Perseverance and Passion for Long-Term Goals." *Journal of Personality and Social Psychology* 92, no. 6 (2007): 1087–1101. https://doi.org/10.1037/0022-3514.92.6.1087.

Dweck, Carol. *Mindset: The New Psychology of Success.* Ballantine Books, 2016.

Emmons, Robert. "10 Ways to Become More Grateful." *Greater Good Magazine,* November 17, 2010. https://greatergood.berkeley.edu/article/item/ten_ways_to_become_more_grateful1.

Ewert, Christina, Annika Vater, and Michela Schröder-Abé. "Self-Compassion and Coping: A Meta-Analysis." *Mindfulness* 12, no. 5 (May 2021): 1063–77. https://doi.org/10.1007/s12671-020-01563-8.

Faller, Mary Beth. "Bob Bowman Uses Michael Phelps to Explain How to Achieve Excellence." *Arizona State University News*, January 30, 2017. https://news.asu.edu/20170130-sun-devil-life-bob-bowman-uses-michael-phelps-explain-how-achieve-excellence.

Forleo, Marie. *Everything Is Figureoutable*. Portfolio, 2019.

Foster, Lilibet, dir. *Be Here Now: The Andy Whitfield Story*. Silver Lining Entertainment, 2015.

Giacobbi, Peter R., Jonathan Stewart, Keeley Chaffee, Anna-Marie Jaeschke, Meagan Stabler, and George A. Kelley. "A Scoping Review of Health Outcomes Examined in Randomized Controlled Trials Using Guided Imagery." *Progress in Preventive Medicine* 2, no. 7 (December 2017): e0010. https://doi.org/10.1097/pp9.0000000000000010.

Godwin, Christine A., Michael A. Hunter, Matthew A. Bezdek, et al. "Functional Connectivity Within and Between Intrinsic Brain Networks Correlates with Trait Mind Wandering." *Neuropsychologia* 103 (August 2017): 140–53. https://doi.org/10.1016/j.neuropsychologia.2017.07.006.

Gold, Andrea L., Rajendra A. Morey, and Gregory McCarthy. "Amygdala–Prefrontal Cortex Functional Connectivity During Threat-Induced Anxiety and Goal Distraction." *Biological Psychiatry* 77, no. 4 (February 2015): 394–403. https://doi.org/10.1016/j.biopsych.2014.03.030.

Hof, Wim. "The Official Wim Hof Method Website." Accessed April 2, 2025. www.wimhofmethod.com.

Iodice, Jo A., John M. Malouff, and Nicola S. Schutte. "The Association Between Gratitude and Depression: A Meta-Analysis." *International Journal of Depression and Anxiety* 4, no. 1 (June 2021): 024. https://doi.org/10.23937/2643-4059/1710024.

Jackowska, Marta, Jennie Brown, Amy Ronaldson, and Andrew Steptoe. "The Impact of a Brief Gratitude Intervention on Subjective Well-Being, Biology and Sleep." *Journal of Health Psychology* 21, no. 10 (October 2016): 2207–17. https://doi.org/10.1177/1359105315572455.

Jain, Vivek, Joseph Marbach, Shawn Kimbro, et al. "Benefits of Oxytocin Administration in Obstructive Sleep Apnea." *American Journal of Physiology–Lung Cellular and Molecular Physiology* 313, no. 5 (November 2017): L825–33. https://doi.org/10.1152/ajplung.00206.2017.

Jankowski, Marek, Tom L. Broderick, and Jolanta Gutkowska. "The Role of Oxytocin in Cardiovascular Protection." *Frontiers in Psychology* 11 (August 2020): 2139. https://doi.org/10.3389/fpsyg.2020.02139.

Johns Hopkins Medicine. "Limb Loss Experts Address an Increasing Need for Amputation Rehabilitation." March 7, 2019. www.hopkinsmedicine.org/news/articles/2019/03/limb-loss-experts-address-an-increasing-need-in-the-us-and-abroad.

Jonikas, Jessica A., Dennis D. Grey, Mary Ellen Copeland, et al. "Improving Propensity for Patient Self-Advocacy Through Wellness Recovery Action Planning: Results of a Randomized Controlled Trial." *Community Mental Health Journal* 49, no. 3 (June 2013): 260–69. https://doi.org/10.1007/s10597-011-9475-9.

Kwik, Jim. *Limitless: Upgrade Your Brain, Learn Anything Faster, and Unlock Your*

Exceptional Life. Hay House, 2020.

Li, William. *Eat to Beat Disease: The New Science of How Your Body Can Heal Itself.* Grand Central, 2019.

Lodi, Ernesto, Lucrezia Perrella, Rita Zarbo, and Patrizia Patrizi. "Courage as Mediator Between Positive Resources and General/Domain-Specific Well-Being Indices." *European Journal of Investigation in Health, Psychology and Education* 12, no. 8 (August 2022): 1067–81. https://doi.org/10.3390/ejihpe12080076.

Maltz, Maxwell. *Psycho-Cybernetics: Updated and Expanded.* Tarcher, 2015.

Mao, Yidi, Jiaxu Zhao, Yi Xu, and Yanhui Xiang. "How Gratitude Inhibits Envy: From the Perspective of Positive Psychology." *PsyCh Journal* 10, no. 3 (June 2021): 384–92. https://doi.org/10.1002/pchj.413.

Neck, Chris P., and Charles C. Manz. "Thought Self-Leadership: The Influence of Self-Talk and Mental Imagery on Performance." *Journal of Organizational Behavior* 13, no. 7 (1992): 681–99. https://doi.org/10.1002/job.4030130705.

Patricolo, Gail Elliott, Amanda LaVoie, Barbara Slavin, Nancy L. Richards, Deborah Jagow, and Karen Armstrong. "Beneficial Effects of Guided Imagery or Clinical Massage on the Status of Patients in a Progressive Care Unit." *Critical Care Nurse* 37, no. 1 (February 2017): 62–69. https://doi.org/10.4037/ccn2017282.

Perkins-Gough, Deborah. "The Significance of Grit: A Conversation with Angela Lee Duckworth." Association for Supervision and Curriculum Development. September 1, 2013. www.ascd.org/el/articles/the-significance-of-grit-a-conversation-with-angela-lee-duckworth.

Pressfield, Steven. *The War of Art: Break Through the Blocks and Win Your Inner Creative Battles.* Black Irish Entertainment LLC, 2012.

Purdy, Amy. "Living Beyond Limits." TED Talk, Orange Coast College, CA, May 2011. 9 min., 35 sec. www.ted.com/talks/amy_purdy_living_beyond_limits.

Purdy, Amy, host. *Bouncing Forward.* Podcast. Season 1, episode 9. "Liz Gilbert on Getting Through the Most Difficult Moments of Life." March 1, 2021. https://podcasts.apple.com/us/podcast/bouncing-forward-with-amy-purdy/id1546895069?i=1000511128119.

Purdy, Amy, host. *Bouncing Forward.* Podcast. Season 1, episode 21. "Hassan Khan: 5 Characteristics of a Resilient Person." April 12, 2021. https://podcasts.apple.com/us/podcast/bouncing-forward-with-amy-purdy/id1546895069?i=1000516793601.

Purdy, Amy, host. *Bouncing Forward.* Podcast. Season 1, episode 31. "Kute Blackson: The Magic of Surrender: Why We Need to Let Go of Control and Let Life Flow." May 25, 2021. https://podcasts.apple.com/us/podcast/31-kute-blackson-the-magic-of-surrender-why-we-need/id1546895069?i=1000522911854.

Purdy, Amy, host. *Bouncing Forward.* Podcast. Season 2, episode 10. "Amy Cuddy: Living Inspired Through Uninspiring Times and the Importance of Supporting One Another." December 20, 2021. https://podcasts.apple.com/us/podcast/bouncing-forward-with-amy-purdy/id1546895069?i=1000545527911.

Purdy, Amy, host. *Bouncing Forward.* Podcast. Season 2, episode 2. "Derek Hough: How to Get Inspired Through Movement and Why Inspiration Is Contagious." November 9, 2021. https://podcasts.apple.com/us/podcast/bouncing-forward-with-amy-purdy/id1546895069?i=1000541261819.

Purdy, Amy, host. *Bouncing Forward.* Podcast.

Season 2, episode 3. "Susie Moore: How to Manage Stress and Let It Be Easy to Live a More Inspired Life." November 15, 2021. https://podcasts.apple.com/us/podcast/bouncing-forward-with-amy-purdy/id1546895069?i=1000541977815.

Redwine, Laura S., Brook L. Henry, Meredith A. Pung, et al. "Pilot Randomized Study of a Gratitude Journaling Intervention on Heart Rate Variability and Inflammatory Biomarkers in Patients with Stage B Heart Failure." *Psychosomatic Medicine* 78, no. 6 (2016): 667–76. https://doi.org/10.1097/PSY.0000000000000316.

Robbins, Mel, host. *The Mel Robbins Podcast.* Podcast. Episode 227. "#1 Neurosurgeon: How to Manifest Anything You Want & Unlock the Unlimited Power of Your Mind." October 24, 2024. www.melrobbins.com/podcasts/episode-227.

Shapiro, Shauna L., Linda E. Carlson, John A. Astin, and Benedict Freedman. "Mechanisms of Mindfulness." *Journal of Clinical Psychology* 62, no. 3 (2006): 373–86. https://doi.org/10.1002/jclp.20237.

Slimani, Maamer, David Tod, Helmi Chaabene, Bianca Miarka, and Karim Chamari. "Effects of Mental Imagery on Muscular Strength in Healthy and Patient Participants: A Systematic Review." *Journal of Sports Science & Medicine* 15, no. 3 (August 2016): 434–50. www.ncbi.nlm.nih.gov/pmc/articles/PMC4974856.

Weigensberg, Marc J., Cheng K. Fred Wen, Donna Spruijt-Metz, and Christianne Joy Lane. "Effects of Group-Delivered Stress-Reduction Guided Imagery on Salivary Cortisol, Salivary Amylase, and Stress Mood in Urban, Predominantly Latino Adolescents." *Global Advances in Health and Medicine* 11 (February 2022): 21649561211067443. https://doi.org/10.1177/21649561211067443.

World Health Organization. "Disability." Fact Sheets. March 7, 2023. www.who.int/news-room/fact-sheets/detail/disability-and-health.

ACKNOWLEDGMENTS

I REALIZE THAT I HAVE ACCOMPLISHED what I have in my life because of the amazing support I've had along the way—from my family to my coaches to my medical team. I may have been the one crossing the finish line, but it took their support to get me to the starting line in the first place. Thank you to everyone who has supported my journey. I wouldn't be where I am today without your love, dedication, and support.

ABOUT THE AUTHOR

AMY PURDY is a three-time Paralympic medalist, trailblazer in the sport of snowboarding, and *New York Times* bestselling author who has been published in ten languages around the world. She is one of the world's most sought-after motivational and corporate speakers and was named one of Oprah's SuperSoul 100 Thought Leaders.

A leader on both resilience and creativity, she is a passionate, visceral storyteller whose onstage presentations "Living Beyond Limits" and "Bouncing Forward" have inspired millions around the globe to take charge of their own lives and rewrite their futures.